MORE LOVE AND SEX

FROM MY MESSY BEDROOM

More Love and Sex
from
My Messy Bedroom

JOSEY VOGELS

Véhicule Press

So many people to thank, so little space...
Thanks to Simon and Vicki at Véhicule Press for all their
hard work; to the many editors who have tweaked my columns
these last four years; to my readers for their letters and kind words;
and to my family and friends for the love, support
and great material.

Cover photograph by Thomas Leon Königsthal, Jr.
Art direction by J.W. Stewart
Cover imaging by André Jacob
Interior designed and typeset by Simon Garamond
Printing by AGMV-Marquis Inc.
Reprinted April 1999

CANADIAN CATALOGUING IN PUBLICATION DATA

Vogels, Josey
More love and sex from my messy bedroom

ISBN: 1-55065-108-0

1. Sex. 2. Love. 3. Man-woman relationships. I. Title.

HQ16.V64 1998   306.7   C98-901117-8

Published by Véhicule Press
P.O.B. 125, Place du Parc Station
Montréal, Québec H2W 2M9

Distributed by General Distribution Services

Printed in Canada on alkaline paper.

Contents

Welcome Back to
My Messy Bedroom...

WHEN I FIRST STARTED started writing "My Messy Bedroom" as a column for *Hour* Magazine in Montreal, the guys at the paper said it wouldn't last. "You're going to run out of things to say within six months," they warned.

Four years, syndication, and approximately 200 columns later, I haven't even begun to run out of things to say.

It's been one of the most fulfilling relationships of my life. I was working as an editor at *Hour* when my boss asked me to come up with a weekly column. I tried to think of something I had enough basic background and interest in to write about every week. Sex seemed an obvious choice. I'd been having it since I was 14—the longest I'd stuck with anything at that point in my life. And while all my smart, funny female friends had lots of opinions about politics and the state of the world, our favourite topic was, and still is, boys and sex.

Some consider this shallow, even frivolous. But one thing I've learned in these last four years is that the struggle to have healthy, happy relationships is not frivolous. The need to have our sexual preferences and choices explained and validated is not shallow.

The hunger for information about sex and relationships, while occasionally inspired by the same curiosity we have about Bill Clinton's sex life, is basically genuine.

Interpersonal relationships and sexual attraction are mind-boggling subjects. We've been anxious, confused and curious about them since the beginning of time. Many of the questions bear repeating with each generation.

When I get a letter from a sixteen-year-old woman who says I've helped her feel more secure in her developing sexuality, I can't help but feel honoured.

Even, or perhaps especially, when my column inspires hatred, it makes me sit up and take notice of my responsibility. I have at least one particularly charming "fan" whose vile diatribes against me and my entire gender, while disturbing, convince me of the need for women to talk about this stuff. As a woman writing about sex, there is resentment. And a certain amount of titillation. I often get strange looks when people meet me for the first time. They expect me to arrive bearing whips and leather, and are either disappointed or pleasantly surprised to find I'm just a regular gal who grew up in the country in small-town Ontario, the eighth child in a Dutch-Canadian, Catholic family.

In the years I've been writing the column, women writing about sex has become a somewhat of a trend. I guess our time had come. "Death to the Patriarchy" just wasn't doing the trick anymore, and the boys seemed to respond more eagerly when we used sex and relationships as the medium for our feminist messages.

It's also, I believe, an extension of our role in relationships. For the most part, we are still the emotional caretakers.

Granted, the men I've heard from over the years lend me hope that this is changing. They've openly shared their thoughts, experiences, questions and confusion. And that's very cool. In fact, my column wouldn't have lasted without the feedback, criticism, appreciation and support from both male and female readers. These four years have certainly been a learning experience for me. The more I write about sex and relationships, the more I question. And the more I realize just how messy the subjects of love and sex can be.

This book gathers together some of the topics I've tackled over the years:

Trying to cope with the single life; learning to keep romance alive; how to cheat without getting caught; finding out exactly what men and women like in bed; life as a professional dominatrix; penis extensions; and finding good porn, to name just a few.

Welcome back to my messy bedroom…

Flying Solo

Parting Ways
Fifty Ways Not to Leave Your Lover

PAUL SIMON made it sound so easy: just hop on a bus, Gus, no need to discuss. But while dropping off the key might have worked for Lee, and slipping out the back made Jack a free man, these guys were cowardly schmucks and would have a hard time getting away with that kinda shit these days. You have to at least try to come up with some sort of pathetic explanation for why you want out. And face it, ending a relationship that ain't cutting it can be a whole lot more complicated than simply makin' a new plan, Stan. Unless the feeling is mutual, and you can make a clean break, you'll find yourself faced with the delicate task of trying to let someone down easy. Truth of the matter is, there's no easy way to do it. And so, I repeat myself, at the risk of being crude, there must be (at least) 50 lame ways to leave your lover.

The "I couldn't be honest with you if I tried" method:
- "It's not you, it's me." *Response*: "No kidding."
- "I don't want to break up but I think we should see other people." *Translation*: I'll sleep with you until something better comes along.

- "Our needs are different right now." *Trans*: You're too needy.
- "You're too needy." *Trans*: I'm too selfish.
- "You're too selfish." *Trans*: I'm too needy.
- "We want different things." *Trans*: You want a relationship and I don't.
- "I'm just not ready to be in a relationship right now." *Trans*: I'm not ready to be in a relationship with you.
- "I'm afraid I'll just end up hurting you." *Response*: What? As opposed to what you're doing now?
- "Maybe we should just be friends." *Trans*: I've started seeing someone else.
- "I don't know what I want." *Trans*: I will never know what I want.
- "Maybe we should take a break." *Trans*: I can't stand you but if I can't meet anyone else I wouldn't mind having you there to sleep with if I'm really desperate.

The "play dumb" method:

- "Whoops, did I really say we'd go out tonight?"
- "I just never expected things to get serious." Trans: I only get involved in pointless relationships.
- "Oh, I didn't realize you wanted me to call you back."

The "looking out for #1" method:

- "Your expectations are too high." *Trans*: You have expectations and I just wanted to have a good time.
- "I think you're getting too attached." *Trans*: I only like to have cold, distant relationships.

♦ "I think it would be the best thing for both of us." *Trans*: I think it would be the best thing for me.

"You're too dependent." *Trans*: You're pathetic.

"You're too independent." *Trans*: I'm pathetic.

"I need space." Trans: I'm terrified of getting close to anyone.

"I can't give you what you want right now." Trans: I need to grow up.

"We can still be friends." *Trans*: We can still have sex when we're drunk.

The "I'm a coward" method:

♦ "You're too good for me. You deserve better." *Response*: Damn right I do, but you're the last person I want to point that out to me.

♦ Dumping anyone long-distance.

♦ Dumping someone via letter, e-mail or answering machine message.

The "punch me in the gut" method:

"You're really nice but I just don't find you sexually attractive." *Response*: "Ouch!"

♦ "I'm moving to Africa."

The "I don't know what I want and I'm going to make you pay for it" method:

♦ "I've changed."

♦ "You've changed."

♦ "It's just that I had dinner with my ex the other night and we've still got feelings for each other." Trans: I'd like to keep you

17

on the side in case things don't work out with the person I really want to be with.

And of course, one of my all-time favourites—"I love you but I'm not in love with you." *Trans*: I don't know what being in love means.

The "just plain lame" method:

- ◆ "I liked your hair better before you cut it."
- ◆ Stop returning phone calls.
- ◆ Don't show up for a date.
- ◆ "It's just not working out." *Trans*: I can't even be creative about dumping you.

Then again, maybe Gus et al. had the right idea.

Past Tense

Can Ex-Lovers Become Friends?

WE WERE READY. And it had only been two months. I was impressed. In some cases, it takes years—sometimes it never happens. Of course, you can't entirely trust it that soon. Yes, my ex and I were testing the waters of—Yikes!—friendship!

We actually managed to hang for a whole day and had a great time, without getting maudlin or ending up in the sack together. There was even alcohol involved. Not bad, eh? It helped that we were on a group outing for the better part of the day. Mind you, there was a touch-and-go period there, when his friends left us alone on a blanket in the park in the sunshine. A true test of will.

I wasn't sure how he'd handle it because we had had conversations during our relationship about being friends with your exes. He's from the old you-can't-be-friends-with-your-ex school. I'm the opposite. I think it's crucial to at least try. It's that new-agey closure thing.

I've got a pretty good track record. I've managed to establish close friendships with all my serious relationships. No, that's not true. One guy got away, but he was a lousy friend during the relationship, anyway. It soon became obvious that my attempts to become buds once it was over were futile. That one still creeps up on me sometimes. Unresolved relationships do that.

That's because becoming friends allows you to clean house—throw out the junk and hang on to the stuff you like. If you don't get to do this, you stay stuck in the relationship as it was—unworkable—even if you don't see each other.

But you can't rush it. You, know, calling after a week "just to talk on the phone—as friends." While part of you welcomes the gesture, something to ease the separation anxiety. Part of you knows you're just putting off the pain.

And we all know what happens when you try to pretend you're over it too soon. It starts on the phone, then you agree to get together. Once face to face, chemistry takes over, you fall for some crap about things being different. It's easy to get sucked in by familiarity and a selective memory. You just slip on your rose-coloured glasses and convince yourself it wasn't so bad—especially if there's nothing on the horizon. Then your sex drive butts in on the conversation and the next thing you know it's morning and you're making coffee for two and suffering a major emotional hangover from falling off the wagon.

And, of course, it's never as good as you imagined it would be when you sleep with an ex. Not just because you were drunk, but because reality has a hard time living up to fantasy and the distance between you makes it impossible to slip back to that space in which you were once so comfortably nestled.

Becoming friends with someone you've been burned by is an

even bigger challenge. You really have to be ready for this. Otherwise it's too easy for the person to push your buttons. You need enough distance and perspective to feel in control.

It always helps if you've been working on some some replacement material.

Not that you're allowed to mention that. Even if you are both able to accept that things won't work out between you, that doesn't mean you're ready to feel replaced. And while it's tempting to thumb your nose at your ex and go "Ha, ha, I've met someone new," out of respect and to avoid feeling like you're suddenly in high school again smugly walking by his locker with a new squeeze, it's best to hold back for awhile. Until you're sure it's safe.

Once you do manage to establish a friendship with an ex, you then get to deal with the joys of how your new relationships handle your friendships with your exes. Whether or not they indulge that little nagging voice in the back of their mind when you tell them you're going for dinner with your ex, that whispers, "What if they get back together?" or at the very least, "What if they sleep together?"

Admittedly, some people make it tough not to feel somewhat suspicious. Especially the ones who define the term friendship rather oddly. More than once, I've had lovers do the 911 emergency service for a fresh ex on the verge of a nervous breakdown. Call me crazy but when I'm on the verge of a nervous breakdown running to one of the contributing factors to my state of mind seems just a little counterproductive.

Of course, these suspicions can be appeased with reassurances that a friendship with an ex is truly just a friendship. Something along the lines of how I am the most wonderful thing in the world and how nothing could shake his undying love for me—might work.

Besides, allowing a date to resolve his or her past relationships, makes them more available to you in the present.

As well as a potentially much happier and well-rounded person. Because really, what could be better than creating a good friend out of someone who knows you intimately. Life's too short and real connections with people too far and few between to be discarded like that. And bonus, you'll have someone else to drag to weddings and bar mitzvahs when your date can't make it.

On the Rebound
How to Bounce Back with Style

I COULDN'T figure it out. I'd been out of my last relationship for over a month, and hadn't jumped into bed with anybody new yet. I'm usually much more efficient at rebounding. So efficient, in fact, I usually like to get a backup or two going ahead of time— y'know, when I realize the relationship is headed for nowheresville but I'm too much of a masochist to get out of it. Having a backup means there's someone already on hand to absorb the blow when you finally do get out. Some people consider this kind of overlapping unhealthy and indicative of someone who is obviously too weak and lily-livered to be alone. Personally, I like to think of it as planning ahead.

I had a backup going for awhile there when things started to sour in my relationship. Unfortunately, the masochist in me was so enjoying the trip to nowheresville, I couldn't keep the heat up on the back burner long enough. The backup backed out before my boyfriend did.

So there I was on the rebound. In search of that wonderfully— if somewhat illusory—restorative romp that renews your faith and catapults you into your new life as a single person. I managed to line up a few possibilities. But this weird thing kept happening—when it got down to actually doing anything about it, I found myself saying, "Naaah, forget it."

On my better days, I thought perhaps this was a sign of maturity. Maybe this time I had managed to come out of a relationship with enough of me intact to not need that shallow, immediate and desperately welcome approval from someone I barely know. More often it was just that I didn't feel like waking up next to someone I barely knew in exchange for an hour or two of superficial satisfaction. On the other hand, I think part of me was just too bloody scared. That particular relationship left me a little worse for wear. I was feeling pretty cynical about the whole pairing up thing. Truth be told, I was considering packing it in. No more relationships. Who needs it?

Of course, everyone around me was saying. Don't lose faith. There are lots of wwwuuunderful men out there. And a nice little fling would do you good—get you over the hump, ease the transition.

I felt it at first. In fact, my first week out, all I wanted was sex—pure, physical, no-strings-attached sex. The ritual replacement. The ceremonial erasing of the memory of "his" warm body in my bed by replacing it with the scent of a complete stranger.

Then it passed. That morning-after thing kept creeping up. You know, you both wake up with serious hangovers, make small talk, hope he doesn't expect breakfast and pretend you'll call each other.

Still, part of me wanted to rebound. Have myself a nice casual fling to get the blood circulating again. It was obvious that I was a little starved for physical affection. At one point, a guy ran his hand across my back in a bar and I practically creamed my jeans.

But I think another part of me was afraid I'd make the ultimate rebound mistake. You know, mistake the casual affection for something more and try and turn it into a relationship or something stupid like that. It's always so tempting. Just pack all your shit from the last relationship and dump it on the first doorstep that comes along. I've seen it plenty. People who jump right into something else and then suddenly, two years down the road, realize that what they thought qualified as a relationship has been little more than a marathon rebound. And as we all know, rebound relationships aren't built to last.

I think there oughta be a rule that once you leave a relationship you must wear a warning sign at all times that reads "On the Rebound." That way, even if you lose sight of your objectives, innocent victims will know what they're getting into and make an informed decision about whether they want to get involved.

Because you know what kinds of things you're in for if you get involved with someone on the rebound. They could still be harbouring revenge fantasies for their ex, and next thing you know you get dragged into ugly scenes involving the ex, jealous rages and flying chairs. Or you could end up with a hardcore rebounder like a friend of mine, who likens her rebound style to a squash game. Chances are, you will be one of several walls off of which she will bounce. And there's always the danger that a rebounder will latch on to you like a lifeboat on the *Titanic*.

I do believe that it is possible to have perfectly fun, honest, no-strings-attached rebound sex—if you're truly, honestly clear that that's all it is. Though just to be on the safe side, it's helpful if one of you is getting ready to leave the country.

If you want to play it a little safer but still get some of the rebound effects you could always stop at crushes and flirting. Crushes work particularly well because they exist entirely in your head and nobody gets hurt. And flirting's great because it gives you that superficial shot in the arm, without the breakfast dilemma the next morning.

Feast or famine
How to Get through the Dry Spells

"Everyone should have to go through a dry spell at some point in their life," Miss Cute-as-a-Button is telling me as I'm half paying attention and half looking around the bar for someone to break my own two-month-old period of involuntary abstinence.

"So what's the longest you've gone?" I ask her, lingering on a red-headed possibility at the pool table.

"A month," she admits rather sheepishly. My rolling eyes prompt her to quickly add, "But I'm still young. I haven't experienced a *real* dry spell yet."

Truth is, women who look like her don't ever have to do without for very long. Not if they don't want to. And who ever really *wants* to go without sex for long periods of time?

"I actually enjoy the occasional dry spell," a friend tells me. "When I don't have sex for a while, I focus on my own stuff." Easy for her to say. She's in a long-term relationship and getting some regularly.

Though theoretically, she's right. As another fellow Not-Getting-Any Club member confides, "Going without sex is great when you get into that phase where you really don't think about it all that much because you are too busy thinking about the story you're writing, what you are going to cook for dinner, what you overheard at a restaurant. Basically, when you get a life."

Inevitably, though, the dull ache in the region from your hips to the tops of your thighs takes over and you find yourself scanning the bar, the subway car—yes, even the laundromat (though it seemed ridiculous when Cosmo suggested it as a great place to meet men). Before you know it, your standards are all out of whack. Suddenly, eighteen-year-olds don't seem like such a bad idea, and bald and paunchy is somehow terribly charming.

It's hard not to correlate the length of time you've gone without sex with how much of a loser you are. That's what makes people so uncomfortable with the question. Two years is pretty much the limit. No one, in my experience, will admit to longer than that.

"My longest dry spell was nine months," another attractive female friend confesses. "It was hell. I became such a mean person, my family was considering taking up a collection to get me some. I was in such a state. I felt like, 'What's wrong with me?' And the wear and tear on my vibrator, I tell ya...."

Obviously, some of us are better at doing without than others. For some, two weeks sends them into a panic. For others, sexlessness is less frightening.

My longest dry spell so far (besides the first fourteen years of my life) is eight months, when I first moved to Montreal to attend university at age twenty-five. Fresh out of a relationship in Toronto, in a new city with no friends and surrounded by eighteen-year-olds, I eventually had no choice. So what if he had to phone his parents afterwards to tell them he was staying "with a friend"? The spell was broken. I had a good run of lovers that summer. Summer's a pretty reliable antidote for dry spells. That's why it's best to time breakups just before summer. It lessens your odds of sexual deprivation.

Now, I realize that sexlessness by choice isn't the same as involuntary abstinence—when you just can't seem to get any no matter how hard you try. (Though if you wait too long, self-imposed abstinence can eventually become involuntary abstinence. Use it or lose it, as they say.)

Unfortunately, people who want some and can't get it are often their own worst liability. You can smell 'em a mile away. Ah, Eau de Desperation. But hey, it's hard not to feel a little desperate when no one seems to want to sleep with you. Especially when, during your time of need, it seems like everyone around is getting laid in abundance. You can almost be forgiven for trying to jump the person who just asked you where the washroom is because, obviously, he or she wants to sleep with you but just hasn't realized it yet.

Cruelly, the only thing that will shake the scent is to get laid. Just once, and suddenly the spell is broken, your confidence returns and you magically become desirable again.

Hopefully, you don't smell too bad by then.

Fling fever
A Mini-relationship without the Mess

MY MOST MEMORABLE summer fling happened several years ago when I was travelling along the east coast. It only lasted two days but they were glorious and besides, two days equals several months in fling years.

We spent them window-shopping, strolling, swimming in the ocean, taking a ferry over to an island, and lounging the afternoon away on the beach. All this, of course, interspersed with lots of passionate public and private displays of affection and completely hot sex.

That's the beauty of a summer fling. You get to enjoy all the awesome things about the beginnings of a relationship but in a fling the possibility of a relationship—possibly due to the fact that he lives on the other side of the world and is leaving the next day—is not usually an option and you both know it. As a result, you can let down your guard and enjoy.

Now, a fling is not to be confused with a one-night-stand. A fling is more like a mini-relationship without all the mess. You don't have to meet his parents, or worry whether your friends will like him. And when you part it's usually circumstance, not the fact that you can't stand to be in the same room together, that splits you up. It still breaks your heart to end it, but the pain doesn't last as long and it's mixed with a warm glow that eventually fades into a fond memory.

After my fling and I parted, I spent a couple days agonizing over whether I should drop everything in my life, jump on the back of his motorbike, and go back to New Zealand with him. After I got over that, we corresponded for almost two years, writing flirtatious letters, thriving on the sexual energy of that two-day encounter. He ended up coming back (sort of a fling follow-up tour of his year-long trip around the world) and, after hanging out with him for a few days on my own turf, I quickly discovered we really were from different worlds.

That's the's the beauty of a fling. Life, along with reality, is temporarily suspended. You end up with people you might not have anything to do with in your real life. If you're both not totally fascinated by everything you have to say to each other it's okay, because you'd rather just have sex anyway.

With a fling, you do things you wouldn't probably let yourself do if it was serious because it would mean too much or you might set a bad precedent. "What, you won't give me four-hour blow jobs every day for the rest of my life!" It's easier to relax and be honest about what you want with a fling because you've got nothing to lose.

This also means that sex can sometimes be kinkier with a fling because inhibitions get dropped. And because being together is purely for pleasure, there is no pressure about where it's going or who's getting more attached.

Flings are a nice break from the great compatibility search. It's easier to ignore differences if you know you're don't have to put up with them for long. Like the fling I once had with an electrician from the suburbs. His uncomplicatedness was like a breath of fresh air from all the angst-ridden urban boys I'd been seeing, but, of course, being an angst-ridden urban girl, I'm sure it would have run its course pretty quickly if we actually tried to have a relationship. As the old saying goes: There's a Mr. Right and a Mr. Right Now.

Flings can work at home too but when you live in the same city, the break usually isn't as clean. Inevitably one of you is gonna decide the fling is over before the other thinks it is. Living in different parts of the world makes things so much easier. Bad timing works well too, like you meet someone just as you're about to leave for the Arctic for a five-year contract on a fishing boat or he's about to join a monastery.

In fact, going away is great for flings. It's easier to completely wrap yourself up in someone when you know you're leaving town. Less risk. Not to say that flings are entirely risk-free. Sometimes you get fooled. You forget that the reason things are so great is the very fact that it's a fling and not a relationship. You have to keep in mind that you're in lust, not love.

Some people have more difficulty with this than others. Number one fling rule: No expectations allowed! You must always be up front about the limitations of what it is you're doing. No "I love you's" after Day Two or silly talk about how you can rearrange your life to spend the rest of it with each other.

For this reason, some might think flings are a waste of time. Why bother if you're not going to have a full relationship, right? But flings are terrific training ground. You can test out different strategies, check out reactions, explore your relationship patterns, try some new moves. Think of it as research.

And finally, there is always that remote possibility that a fling does somehow turn into a relationship. The great thing about this if it does happen is that you've already established a good base of low expectations.

But mostly, flings are just fun. They're the ideal summer sport. And they can leave you with a glow that just might get you through the winter.

The Single Life
Some of Us Just Aren't Cut Out for It

YOU KNOW THE ONES. They're like vacuum cleaners—they come with an attachment. They probably came out of their mother's womb in a couple. I have a friend like this. In our entire ten-year friendship, I have never known her to be single for more than, say, a week. Two consecutive Saturday nights home alone sends her into a panic.

Okay, I admit, I prefer something to squeeze beside my zits and while I may pronounce with seeming pride and independence that "I'd rather be alone," it's usually more for show or to save face when I've just been totally jerked around by someone.

Still, I maintain—whether voluntary or not—a few stretches of the blissful single life is good for you. You know, the life we wax nostalgic over when we're in a relationship conveniently forgetting, of course, all the money we spent hanging out in bars constantly on the lookout, pretending we're really enjoying ourselves, then going home empty-handed night after night because everyone knows you're way more attractive when you're already in a couple.

What was I saying about the occasional bout of singledom being good for you? Oh yeah, they provide proof that you do have the capacity to make it alone. I'm still here, after all.

There's no rule saying a certain amount of time out between relationships is required, or that if you put in so much time on your own your next relationship will be better (I've got proof for that one too).

But it makes me nervous. Take my friend. She attracts men easily. "Why wouldn't you," I tell her—you're smart, gorgeous, funny, etc. But she still gets sucked in by the attention and ends up hurling herself into one mediocre relationship after another. "What do you want me to do," she argues. "It feels artificial to actively avoid a possible involvement." Hey, telemarketers seek me out like flies to well, you know, and I have no problem going out of my way to avoid them despite their promises for money, happiness and other neat stuff.

Self-esteem issues aside, apart from being just plain exhausting, constant coupledom allows no time or distance to step back and gain perspective on your relationship behaviour. Goodness knows, you can't see diddley squat when you're in the heat of it.

Admittedly, starting a new relationship fresh on the heels of an old one is useful in certain circumstances. The rebound, as I mentioned earlier, while often unfortunate for the person you get involved with due to your psychopathic tendencies, sometimes is the only thing that will help you move on, especially if the person you're trying to get over treated you like shit. No amount of friendly "he was slime, anyway" advice works as well as some fresh "whew, I'm not a total loser" attraction.

My biggest objection to this behaviour pattern is what I believe to be at the heart of it: that old "I would rather date John Tesh than be alone," feeling.

Sheer terror about being alone makes you settle for less than what you really want, need or deserve in a relationship. Why deal with yourself when you can find something out there to keep you at least mildly interested? "Have you met my new distraction, I mean, boyfriend?"

Keeping It Together

A Fishy Tale
Fairy Tale Love

I FINALLY saw *The Little Mermaid*. It wasn't my choice. He insisted. Something about falling for little Fin Legs last time he was at Disney World. Yes, he was a grown man at the time. "She appeared like a vision amongst the Plutos and Goofys," his story goes. He liked her shells.

Not to worry, I'll sort that out with him on my own.

It's the movie I want to talk about here.

While I'm as much a sucker as the next kid for a little singing, dancing marine life and I know it's Disney but helloooo....

Never mind the perversity of *The Little Mermaid* as a sixteen-year-old animated bombshell, complete with cleavage, waif waist, plenty of midriff, those terrifying doe-y eyes and a mane of hair any Playboy Bunny would envy (just how does she keep her lipstick on under water, anyway?). Let's just look at the story for a second here, shall we? Little Miss Fish Fins decides she's in love with a human, a guy she met for all of three seconds when he was half unconscious (then again, sounds a bit like my early dating years).

Now, in order to be with him she has to give up her entire world, leave her family and sacrifice her voice. Freshly mute, she has three days to make Prince Stud fall in love with her. But what girl needs to speak when she's got those looks, that body and, "Don't forget to bat your eyelashes," her handlers advise. Right. There's a healthy message for the new generation of little girls clawing at their parents to "Buy me the video, puhllleeeeze!, then buy me the doll, the poster, the pencil case and the $300 plastic underwater sea world complete with all the characters....": It takes about thirty seconds to fall in love; if you want him, just sit pretty and don't talk, and after three days, give up your whole world to marry him and you'll live happily every after.

The message for the boys is great too. Prince Boy sits around waiting for "The One" to suddenly appear, like a vision (wearing a shell bra). "She's out there. I'll just know it when I meet her." Like we need more hopeless romantics out there holding out for effortless love.

No wonder we're so screwed up.

We're still raised on fairy-tale love, when really, the fairy tales have it all wrong. And I'm not trying to be cynical here. I've just let myself "fall" in love one too many times. Maybe I am just cynical but, the truth is, love really isn't something you fall into at all. It's something you build over time. They make it look so easy in the fairy tales. That's where we get messed up. And when there's suddenly some effort involved, we go hey, that can't be love, no one said there was work involved.

But it's not work. It's the pleasure of discovering someone, truly getting to know them, the good and the bad, and the ugly.

Beyond the initial flush.

I'm now leery of people who talk love too soon. You don't know me, I think. We mistake strong mutual attraction for love. We think that's enough. But that's only the beginning. The thing that starts you on the path, the one that leads to the possibility of love.

But we're impatient. We're struck and before we know it we have the rest of our lives together mapped out according to our own fantasy.

Don't get me wrong, I love the rush of meeting someone who really turns your crank. It's a wonderful thing when you click with someone and I'm all for pursuing it. I may even bat an eyelash or two just to get the ball rolling. I'm not about to give up my whole world for someone. Until I'm sure he's up to the task of loving me.

I wanna see the sequel, *The Little Mermaid II*, when things fall apart because they realize they know nothing about each other and she lets herself go because she's miserable in this unfamiliar world, he loses his patience with her and has an affair with a younger mermaid.

Keeping Romance Alive
You Don't Bring Me Flowers Anymore

I KNEW it was gone. I remember the precise moment I realized it. I was in the bath—a bubble bath, complete with candlelight. How could he resist, I thought. He walked in, looked at me with something just shy of indifference, uttered something about some work he had to do, and walked out.

My heart, along with my stab at recapturing the romance in our relationship, sank in the warm, bubbly water. Tears sprung to my eyes.

"What's wrong," he asked, my dull sobbing having drawn him back into the bathroom. The question made my heart sink deeper. How could he not know? How could I explain how his reaction, or lack thereof, to such a potentially romantic encounter crushed me—how I wanted him to be swept away by the sight of my nakedness languishing in the candlelit bubbles. How could he not want to tear his clothes off, slide in to the water and make love to me. I wanted him to scrub my back, wash my hair for me, tell me how beautiful I am. I certainly wasn't about to ask…I shouldn't have to, should I?

I had to face it. The romance in our relationship had up and left. I don't know where it went or why. I didn't know why he suddenly no longer felt the need, compulsion or desire to leave sexy messages on my voice mail, bring me breakfast in bed, leave notes on the bathroom mirror. To appreciate me. But, damn it, I wanted it back.

I went at him with cries of "Why can't you be more romantic?" and other variations on the theme.

He came back with different tones of, "If I'm being romantic because you've asked me to, it won't feel natural."

Right, romance isn't something you should have to work at. It should just come naturally. Of course, in that blissful state at the beginning of a relationship, passion and romance come as easily as breath. When it doesn't, we are immediately tempted to believe that there is something terribly wrong with the relationship. But how natural is romance really?

If you look up romance in the dictionary the definition is rife with clues of its artificiality. It is described as, "fanciful, idealized love, dreamy, poetic, impractical…"

Maybe it is a silly notion, romance—or just a fantasy. Maybe we've all watched too many movies, read too many happy endings, listened to too many love songs.

The Mehinaku tribe of central Brazil think a display of romantic love is foolish, and in poor taste. "Excessive thought of a loved one, they believe, can attract deadly snakes, jaguars, and malevolent spirits," writes anthropologist Helen Fischer. Anyone who has been burned by love can attest to this.

Still we crave it. Romance makes you feel special, beautiful, important, worthy, loved, powerful. Who wouldn't want that. And more importantly, who wouldn't want the person they love to feel like that, even if it means acting a little unnatural sometimes.

It's hard to know why, when or how romance fades in a relationship, but it usually does. It's easy at first, in the initial rushes of love, when you're trying to make an impression. But romance doesn't stick around on its own. Work, stress, kids, familiarity, and plain old taking things for granted gets in its way. That's when romance takes effort, imagination, and yes, feeling foolish and even, god forbid, unnatural.

"There is no such thing as love, only proof of love," is a favourite quote of a good friend of mine. And sometimes the proof is in the, uh, putting yourself out.

So next time you find her languishing in the bath....

Verbal Skills

Learning the Fine Art of Communication

"He doesn't talk about his feelings."
   "I never know what he's really *thinking."*
   "He's distant."

Women, myself included, are always complaining about men's inability to communicate. When Deborah Tannen described men's communication style as "report talk" and women's as "rapport talk" in her 1990 book *You Just Don't Understand: Women and Men in Conversation*, we all sighed a collective "I told you so."

It gave us the green light to badger men into talking about how they felt, trying every possible tactic to make them believe that if only they let their emotions flow our relationships would be better. I tend to go the "What are you feeling?" route, a question I inject at regular intervals, while I'm purging my brain of every single thought it can come up with—or when there is one of those uncomfortable quarter-second lulls in the conversation.

With most of the men I've been with, this question usually succeeds only in drawing a blank stare. Every once in a while a guy might humour me and, with furrowed brow, try desperately to come up with an answer. More often than not the answer is, "I don't know... I just don't know what I'm feeling."

That really sets me off. "How can you not know what you're feeling! Why can't you guys communicate?! You'd feel so much better if you talked about things! I'm sick of being the one who does all the emotional work in this relationship..." yadda, yadda, yadda.

At this point, guys who have trouble communicating will do one of two things: they'll withdraw into a tiny little emotional ball never to come out again, or they'll lie because he really *doesn't* know what he is feeling and since I'm constantly telling him that he *should* be feeling something, he'll make something up.

Mind you, it's not much better when he *does* actually communicate. Because he usually doesn't say what I wanna hear, anyway— not that I don't try to make him.

I admit that sometimes my idea of communication is something along the lines of: He finally says something, I get defensive and tell him what's wrong with what he thinks, then he clams up and I get angry because he won't talk about what's wrong. Not exactly the most inviting environment in which to be disclosing your inner-most thoughts. Communication is difficult at the best of times. When someone is silent it's hard not to feel like you're being left out in the cold. It's tempting to fill that silence with your worst fears and wild interpretations of what *might* be going on.

On the other hand, it's hard to speak up when someone's ready to pounce on anything you say. And with all this crowding both your brains, chances are, no one's doing much listening to whatever does get said. I think in a lot of cases what we often mistake as communication is a lot of nodding and uh-huhing in all the right places while our minds are busy plotting out our strategies. It becomes a game of reaction versus reaction, and who can be more right.

It's tough to get it into our heads sometimes that our partner is different from us, and it's amazing the lengths we'll go to get someone to think like us or to see things our way.

Real communication is about being a good talker, recognizing that there's a time and place to discuss things and that your partner's time and place might be different from yours. But, probably even more so, it's about being a good listener. That means not always having to be right and biting your tongue once in a while, even when you feel you might burst if you don't say something in your own defence.

Now, what do you have to say about that?

Feeling Green
When Jealousy Strikes

IT CAUGHT me by surprise. I forgot how ugly it is. I'd forgotten the way it burns. I'm talking about jealousy—that lovely feeling in the pit of your gut fueled by panic, anger, insecurity and a sudden urge to take the eyes out of the woman who has suddenly, perhaps quite innocently, come between you and him. (Of course, to you her innocence is merely a facade for her completely malicious scheming to steal your squeeze.) Yes, jealousy is nasty and not very sisterly.

I guess part of me was naive enough to think that maybe I was past it, that it was kidstuff. Not that I was beyond it, one of those scary-alien types who proclaim, "I don't get jealous." Just that I was beyond succumbing to its irrationality. Then it smacked me upside the head, and the familiar sensation came flooding back.

As usual, its entry, while gale-like in force, was triggered by a simple and barely significant event. A message in a birthday card to my date from a woman (his neighbour) thanking him for letting her use his shower. My date had failed to mention this small gesture and I could have sworn her thank-you had a nudge-nudge-wink-wink tone to it. I was certain there was more to it than good neighbourliness.

Of course, it helped that I already suspected my date of having lascivious thoughts about this woman. This was merely my proof. You don't want to know, I fiercely told myself, though every fibre in my body was crying out for details. Be cool, I muttered to myself, as I calmly inquired as to what she might be referring in her quaint little personalized message.

I didn't like the look I got. I walked away. You simply don't want to hear this, I thought. I came back. He explained, and it reeked of innocence and logic. Which, of course, only made me more suspicious.

After all, if he was so innocent, why had he neglected to mention this little "favour he had done for a friend in need." He did a pretty good selling job, I have to admit, but didn't he realize that withholding evidence is akin to admitting guilt.

"I knew you'd read something else into it if I told you," he explained. Yeah, duh... So should I? Be reading something else into it it, that is? No, he insisted. Honest? No. End of exchange. That's all I'm supposed to need, right. I trusted him, didn't I?

So why did I find myself eyeballing his apartment the next time I was there, scanning for clues, and an opportune moment to rummage through his bedside drawer and count the condoms?

Why was I dividing my time between wondering and trying to stop myself from wondering, occasionally letting my imagination take off, just to see how bad I could feel? And then there were the little films I played in my mind. If he did sleep with her, was it better, did he did try that little thing on her that he had learned I like? Eeeew! Nausea. Stop it!

Okay, I think, if I'm not gonna let myself dig for details, I'll just fish around to see if there's been any further contact. ("Oh, sounds like the party you went to when I was away last weekend was fun, so, who-all went?")

Then I'll waste my time making mental lists of all the things that make me way more interesting than her. And when I'm through the run-down of her flaws, I'll compare body parts.

In a fit of maturity, I get a grip. C'mon, I tell myself, you've had your share of lascivious thoughts and even acted on some. Where do you get off being jealous? He didn't even do anything (or so he says, I slip in). Besides, even if he did, you have to focus on whether it affects your relationship. This is about you and him, not her, I tell myself.

Yeah, but it's not the same when *I* have crushes, or flirt, or even sleep with someone else, I argue back. I know what it means when *I* do it. This rationale is a perfect example of just how irrational jealousy is.

In the end, I think my date was telling the truth, but I'm sure there was some part of him that wanted to keep me in suspense. After all, jealousy can be flattering. But this is where you have to be careful. Jealousy is not a toy.

It may be fun to make someone a little jealous, to keep things on edge and to remind him once in a while of how totally irresistible you are, but making a habit out of deliberately making someone jealous is mean, stupid, and eventually very annoying. Even if it's totally innocent, revealing that you've always fantasized about sleeping with your partner's best friend or constantly commenting on how cute you find so-and-so at the office, or how great your last lover was, may make your partner feel threatened, so think before your speak.

On the other hand, as much as you'd like to think that your date isn't allowed to have had a life before you, you have to put your ego aside and not let yourself get into a flap over every potential threat.

Especially if you're drunk. Drunken jealousy is particularly unsightly, even more so if you're at a party and decide to involve the party guests and selected food items from the buffet table. Avoid.

This is where jealousy slips down the slope into possessiveness (another ugly side of this delightful emotion) which usually succeeds in pushing the person even further away. Right off the planet in some cases. Jealousy is one of the leading causes of domestic violence, including murder. Not a bad thing to keep in mind.

Cheat Sheet

Do It Right or Don't Do It at All

I WALKED right into it. "So did anything actually ever happen between you and her," I asked, once my suspicions had safely dulled. "No, in fact, I'm proud to say I have always been faithful to you," he announced. Silence. The face suddenly staring at me, eyebrows cocked, was obviously returning the question, "Well….how about you?"

I felt like a deer caught in the headlights.

"Well, uh…," my brain did a quick rundown of what amongst my generally flirtatious behaviour during our two-year less-than-solid relationship, constituted cheating. "There was this one time…," I slowly replied, finally settling on a little fling that still carried some weight. I figured, if there were others, and I'm not saying there were, but if there were, they didn't mean anything. Why stir things up more than necessary, right?

Besides, the real issue was why I did it, wasn't it?

That was easy. It was all his fault, of course. He hadn't exactly gone out of his way to make me feel secure in our relationship, he wasn't giving me enough attention, and he was the one who wouldn't go out with me and my friends, leaving me open to temptation.

What's a girl to do? I thought I was being pretty clever. Suddenly, it wasn't about my behaviour, it was about his, and us.

To his credit, he didn't get defensive, or even angry. The most I could get out of him was *maybe* a few pangs of jealousy. I guess I hoped for a little more drama. It figures: the one time I'm up for a little irrational behaviour, he decides to come through and talk out a problem maturely. I was tempted to throw in a few juicy details, to try and get more of a rise out of him, but I held back.

So why *had* I done it? In fact, fidelity has never been my strong point. A similarly fidelity-challenged friend and I have spent many hours on this one. Why was it that in every relationship we'd been in, we eventually succumbed to temptation and fooled around? Insecurity? Approval? Were we going out with guys who weren't fulfilling our needs? Maybe it is simply in our nature? We like that last one. There has even been some recent scientific studies to back us up. Infidelity may be in our genes, they say. Then again, some would say the urge to kill is natural too. And I've so far managed to avoid acting on that one. According to my date's take on foolin' around, apparently, I simply lacked willpower and con-viction.

"As soon as I'm involved with someone, the option is simply ruled out," he tells me matter-of-factly. Wow! I was impressed. Not convinced, mind you, but impressed. His approach seemed so simple. Too simple. I was suspicious. Where does he store all those feelings? How could he put all his eggs in one basket like that? What if someone better comes along and you miss the boat because you were being so faithful? And what about all those other great reasons why you find your eyes darting around the bar or flirting heavily with someone you've just met?

Okay, so you might be secretly trying to sabotage your relationship, or trying to to fill a void in your less-than satisfactory relationship that you're too much of a coward to leave or don't want to work on because it's much easier to jump in bed with someone new to recapture the spark and sexual energy you and your date used to have.

But there's all that good stuff too. Truth of the matter is, sex with someone new can be fun—a quick thrill. Sure it's risky. But so is diving out of planes. And some people are crazy enough to do that.

Having someone take an interest in you, when your date temporarily loses sight of what a truly wonderful person you are, can be ego-building. And doesn't he or she always like you better when you're feeling confident?

Oh sure, you can get some of these benefits without going the full nine yards. In fact, allowing a certain amount of safe flirting is healthy for a relationship. No one can satisfy all your needs. Better to accept the fact that you both like a certain amount of attention outside the relationship than repress it and eventually fall off the wagon, I suppose.

But, if you simply can't resist, and you do fall off the wagon, I have a few words of advice. Consider it my cheat sheet:

Cover your tracks. This includes keeping tabs on your condom supply, stray underwear, and other personal items left behind by your affair. In fact, this is best avoided by staying at his place as often as possible. You avoid the risk of having your mate drop by unexpectedly and you can use that old excuse from high school when you don't make it home some nights. "I stayed at Judy's."

Monitor your behaviour. Guilt-induced behaviour, like suddenly volunteering to do your boyfriend's laundry or wash his floors, will make him suspicious.

Be discreet. Hanging out with your side-dish in open-window cafés staring all googly-eyed at each other in your boy-friend's neighbourhood is probably not a good idea.

Pace yourself. Juggling two (or more) lovers, a job, friends, laundry and the occasional meal can be exhausting.

Pick your affairs carefully. You don't want to have an affair with someone who's suddenly gonna show up on your doorstep at 3 a.m. professing his love for you. Especially when you're in bed with your mate. ("I don't know, dear, some nutcase obviously.")

Learn to lie. Consider it protecting him from the truth, for now, anyway, until you decide what's gonna happen. You don't want to jeopardize things, if it turns out to be meaningless.

Know when to end it. If you're simply in it for a quick boost to your self-esteem, some fun, or to feel really clever, don't let things go on too long. It's bound to get complicated, and then the affair might start pressuring you to make decisions, blah, blah, blah.... This selfish indulgence is about you. Let things get complicated and you'll end up miserable and realize you're not so clever after all, defeating the whole purpose.

Consider the consequences. What's at stake if you're caught? This is a heavy one and often the first thing tossed out the window when it comes to affairs (abandon is half the excitement, after all), but it might be worth a moment of your time. But if you're with someone who's less than open-minded about these things and might not be able to pick up the pieces if he does find out, you might want to think twice. Then again, what are you doing with someone like that anyway? Yes, affairs are a great workout for your rationalization skills.

Deal with the confrontation. If confronted, again, the-whole-truth-and-nothing-but-the-truth credo is best avoided. Almost the truth is enough. No use putting you both through unnecessary pain with extraneous details. Then duck.

Movin' in
The Do's and Don'ts of Shacking Up

I KNEW it was risky. There I was, moving in with someone who doesn't buy the boys-put-the-toilet-seat-down argument. ("What's the difference if I have to put it up, or you have to put it down?" he contended.) I couldn't wait for my first 4 a.m. dip.

Toilet manners was our biggest area of conflict. The second morning in the new place he came into the bedroom with a roll of toilet paper and announced another of his pet peeves. "I like the toilet paper to come out over the top, like this," he said, illustrating his point with a brief demonstration.

Discovering all the annoying habits the other person has managed to keep hidden from you when you lived apart is just one of the joys of moving in together. Who knew he liked to clip his toenails at the breakfast table? The thing is that, however romantic and wonderful the idea of building a cozy little nest together—no matter how much you love 'em, it's still gonna annoy you when he doesn't clean up after himself, or doesn't clean the hair out of the bathtub after his bath.

It's best to point out annoyances as they occur, no matter how petty. (Discovering how truly petty you both can be about things that annoy you is another great moving-in-together discovery.) If you don't they will only fester. If it's not too big a deal, you can probably be accommodated. At the very least you can use the info to piss the other person off. (Did I forget to flush again, dear? So-o-o-o sorry.)

And since nothing's sacred once you share living space, it's also a good idea to be comfy with each other's bodily functions before you move in. I met a woman once, who, after ten years of marriage, had never farted in front of her husband. Brings a tear to yer eye, don't it?

Oh I know, there are folks out there who still object to this living-in-sin bit. And others who think living together is a cop-out, a way to avoid the big "M." But as far as I'm concerned, I couldn't imagine getting married without living with someone first. If I'm supposedly gonna spend the rest of my life with somene, I wanna at least know if he leaves his dirty underwear lying around. And, to be honest, living together is plenty enough commitment for me. As for the cop-out argument, if things get that bad, a piece of paper's not gonna keep me in it. Why make it worse by adding a messy divorce to the break-up? Besides, according to the statistics, shacking up together has become de rigeur.

When we first discussed moving in together, my boyfriend kept referring to it as "the pressure cooker." As in, nothing like living together to find out if this thing is gonna fly. I wasn't big on the analogy. There was enough pressure, what with the toilet-seat debate and all. But it's true, in a way. In many cases, living together—

like marriage—can make or break a relationship.

That's because moving in together forces you to confront the really important issues in life, like who has the ugliest lamps. To be on the safe side, no matter how hideous the vase/mugs/curtains, don't blurt out "Where the hell did you get this ugly thing?!" Chances are, his mother made it. And remember, some things may have sentimental value. I found this out when I suggested his Supersmurf mug might be less than necessary.

The fact that you suddenly have two of everything also makes for some harsh decision making ("Yes, I know your toaster looks better than mine, but mine works.") Amalgamating your belongings can be a good thing—you get to get rid of your crap and use his much better stuff. And sometimes this means you now own things you didn't have before, like a toaster that works.

When you finally do manage to combine your things into some sort of peaceful, if odd, coexistence, you can't help but get a twinge of the agony that will ensue if and when things screw up and you decide to move apart. ("No, I'm sure that orange extension cord was MINE!")

By the way, speaking from experience, moving into one or the other person's place is not recommended, as it will feel like an overextended sleepover. Find a brand-new place together that you can make sufficiently neutral (one trip to Ikea should take care of that).

Preferably a place with a room of one's own. Because the first thing you will want to do after settling into your place together is to get away from each other. I've always thought separate apartments on the same floor with a connecting doorway would be the ultimate solution. Oh, and for your own safety, you might want to lock up your old letters and diaries.

There are good things about moving in together: no more shuffling home to your apartment at 9 a.m.; the thrill of having them bring you fresh-squeezed orange juice (for about the first week, anyway), and having sex wherever you want without fear of a roommate walking in. On the down side, mind you, no more draggin' strangers home for a one-night stand—unless your "new roommate" wants to join in.

Present Tense
It's the Thought that Counts, and Don't You Forget It

WE TEND to measure the quality of our relationships on silly things like how good the sex is, the level of communication, whether you share the same values.... But, when Christmas or a birthday rolls around, we're all reminded of the true test of a relationship—giving each other presents.

The etiquette of gift giving in relationships isn't always obvious. Particularly when it's early in a relationship or the holiday season shows up before you've actually identified whatever it is that is going on between you *as* a relationship. Emily Post never included a rule for how many times you have to sleep with someone before they warrant a Christmas present.

And, should you decide to take the risk and give a gift to someone you've just started seeing, *what* you get them can be even more revealing. Something too personal might have too much meaning; something impersonal might not have enough. Something too generic is, well, too generic. Something too practical lacks romance; something too romantic is too risky.

Spending too little seems cheap; spending too much is extravagant.

Before you know it, an innocent little gift has taken on the ability to define a relationship faster than you can say, "I hope you kept the receipt."

A friend of mine learned this lesson last Christmas. The guy she was seeing was about to leave the country for at least a year, but, despite their attempts to avoid getting too involved before he left, they did, and she felt strongly enough about him to want to give him a Christmas gift. "I put a lot of effort and thought into a gift for him. When I gave it to him, he said he felt bad because he hadn't got me anything. Of course, I told him it didn't matter, but inside I felt like I'd been kicked in the stomach."

Yes, despite all that "to give is better than to receive" crap, when you're seeing someone, giving *without* receiving sucks. It screams "Obviously, I care more about you than you do about me."

Sometimes, a bad gift can be very telling. Once, a guy gave me a pair of sparkly, plaid Converse running shoes for Christmas after we had been going out (and I use the term loosely) for less than a month. Trust me, I'm not a sparkly plaid kinda gal, even back then. In fact, I'm not even a running-shoe kinda gal. Right then, I knew it wasn't to be. I thanked him politely and shoved them into the charity-bound bag in the back of my closet. I dumped him a few weeks later.

But the politics of gift giving isn't lost only on the newly united. Even if you've been together for years, gift giving can speak volumes about the relationship.

Remember, "It's the thought that counts." As in, the amount of thought you put into giving your loved one a Christmas gift will directly reflect how much thought you put into the relationship.

When it comes to gifts for that special someone, you will be tested on the following criteria: uniqueness, originality, how much trouble you went to and your ability to pick up on the subtle hints she's been throwing your way for the last six months.

That drives me nuts. No matter how much I ogle, coo and fawn over things when we're out, begin every second sentence with "I really need/want...," the people I go out with always seem to think they know what I want/need better than I do and they never get me any of the things I've been slobbering over. Either that or they just don't listen.

Pay attention, for God's sake. Especially when it comes to clothing. Rule of thumb, anything *you* think would look good on them is probably a bad idea. You don't want to find yourself in the position of asking, "Honey, how come you never wear that lime-green sweater dress I bought you?"

The day I meet a man who can buy good lingerie, I will marry him. And sorry guys, but those cheesy, butt-riding, scratchy, cheap lace teddies don't qualify.

Buying women household appliances is also to be avoided, as far as I'm concerned. "Oh wow, a new washing machine. This will make doing all your filthy laundry so much more fun. Gee, thanks, dear."

And you don't have to spend big bucks. Use your imagination. In fact, you could save yourself a lot of stress and potential disappointment and both agree to scrap the whole gift thing altogether. Get a bottle of wine, some take-out, unplug the phone and spend all that shopping time in bed together for the day.

Now there's a good gift.

Feelin' Sexy

Guys Talk
What Turns Them On?

"I LIKE A MOUTH on my penis, a hand on my jewels, a finger in my bum, and her looking at me."

Uh, would you like fries with that?

Now here's a guy who know what he likes. I like that. So many guys I've been with, when asked the $64,000 question, "What would you like me to do to/for you," can barely choke up a "What you're doing is great." (A nice ego boost, but not very helpful in terms of direction.) More often I've gotten a barely audible "I don't know."

These days, while women are busy chattering away about what they want, making female orgasm a mandatory part of the curriculum and practically hauling charts into bed mapping out their G-spots, we hear very little about what men like. Do you like your testicles squeezed or cupped? What makes for a blow-you-away blow job? And then there's the matter of the male G-spot.

And judging from the men I talked to, many guys still aren't used to talking about what makes them go wild. "I like to have sex," one particularly forthcoming subject revealed.

Mark, Nathan, John, Jamie, Richard, Pierre, Raoul and Keith all agreed on one thing: men are tiring of their role as initiator. High on the priority list for all these men was a woman who could take charge, or at the very least be an active participant in sex. "Passive women are a big turn-off. I get bored and start thinking about the dripping tap, says Pierre."

"A woman who really takes control and initiates, and not just at the beginning but right through, is a real turn-on," admits Mark.

And not just in bed.

"A woman who recognizes the power of her sex is a real turn-on," says Nathan. Clothes, or the lack of, can be very sexy, he says. "A woman who's wearing no bra or panties and has that I-know-how-much-this-messes-you-up...enjoy! attitude really sends me over the edge."

But, there's a catch. "I want her to be aggressive but still feminine," admitted Keith.

Next to sexual confidence, good oral skills score high. Hey, you try and figure it out when you're fifteen and all you've got to go on is that it's called a "blow" job. Not one of the guys I talked to so much as mentioned blowing on their willie as part of the makings of good oral sex, though "lots of tongue and lips and sucking and stroking at same time" was unanimously appreciated, with "the tongue as the key" being an oft-echoed sentiment. "The butterfly technique is good," Jamie tells me. "That is, flicking your tongue underneath and below the head of the penis."

"It's not a lozenge," impressed Keith. "There needs to be friction." Hands are welcome in the process. "Make a sign for 'perfect' with your forefinger and thumb and use that along with your tongue. I like that."

And keep things moving. "A minute of tongue around the head, some deep throating, then back to something else really holds my attention," explains Richard.

As for teeth, most advise against. "I don't want to be Bobbitted," warns Raoul. If you must nibble, proceed with caution. But the key, they all emphasized, is to at least look like you're enjoying yourself. "Ideally, it should seem like she's enjoying it as much as I am," Nathan offers. "Treat it like a meal. And don't be too goal-oriented—the point is not solely to get me off (though that's obviously nice). Pretend it's the first time you've seen a penis and really explore it." Change in locale is also welcome, he adds. "Sure I'm cooking dinner but… mmmm!"

If you do manage to get him off orally—much appreciated, by the way—there's the question of what to do with "The Milkshake of Life." Yes, some boys like it when you swallow. As for spreading his seed elsewhere on a woman's body, Jamie admits that while an an accidental shot in the eye can be funny, "cumming on a woman is loaded with all this power/domination crap. It's never really done it for me. I mean I don't think I'd want a cum facial either."

Others like to have a little fun with cum.

"It's a cheesy porn thing," speculates John. "I can pretend I'm (porn star) Ron Jeremy for a second.

"But it can also be an intimate, funny thing," he continues. "Cumming on her stomach or back can be kinda cute. You can measure quantity, distance, consistency. And besides, it comes off skin more easily than the sheets."

Being comfy with cum is good," insists Nathan.

"One girl I went out with couldn't get enough of the stuff, and knowing she wanted to see, taste and feel it made me a lot more comfortable with my own needs," he adds.

Men's testicles are sort of a mixed bag, you could say. Neither men or women, it seems, can come to any kind of conclusion as to what to do with them. "They're not like tennis balls: you don't squeeze them as hard as you can," says Jamie. "And they're not like those Chinese exercise balls that you spin around and around in your hand. I don't like that. I prefer cupping and gentle rubbing."

It's not hard to see why we're confused, however.

"You know those Chinese exercise balls that you spin around in your hand?" asks Raoul. "I like it when a women plays with my balls like that."

Go figure.

Everyone but John—who prefers women to avoid his scrotum completely—praised the benefits of oral stimulation, particularly at the base of the scrotum and along the perineum to the butthole, the area Jamie refers to as the "chin rest."

"Of course," he warns, "the concern here is that you might accidentally slip into the nether region that is your anus and, as far as I'm concerned, you don't want to go there."

As with most things sexual, one man's poison is another man's passion—or something like that. Mark, for example, says his butt canal is home of the magic button, and a properly inserted index finger at just the right moment triggers orgasm almost immediately.

What separates the butt boys from the anti-butt boys seems to be a matter of, uh, ease and comfort. "The embarrassment potential turns me off," says Keith.

"One finger is okay, though not too far," says Raoul.

Nipples also got mixed reviews. "I can't even have my nipples touched," says Jamie. "I'm very ticklish, and I get too jumpy."

"I have zero sensitivity in my nipples," says Keith. "I can't feel a thing."

Perhaps it's in the approach. According to Nathan, "the really talented girls know we like attention focussed on our nipples—kissing, licking, biting, pinching...Yes!"

Mark admits that on a purely physical level, men's nipples are probably not all that sensitive, but says it's the psychological connection of having his nipples played with that turns him on. As for John, he'd rather have his toes sucked any day. "They're much more sensitive than my nipples."

In fact, exploring other body parts is highly encouraged, as far as Nathan is concerned. "I like a slow journey across my bodily landscape using fingers, hands, tongue, breasts, nose, anything," he says. "The trick is to know when to stop exploring and settle in a little more heavily. Not everyone gets it right. The best sex partners are the ones who have an intuition about what I want next. 'Yesssss

God, do it again!' is usually a pretty good hint."

"I have an ear fetish," admits Keith. "I love to be nibbled along the ears."

"And my hair! I love having my hair played with," emphasizes Raoul.

Forget all this wimpy fondling, says John. "The most exciting thing is to be a little scared, not soft music and touching for an hour. I like risk. I like it when there's the potential to get caught."

And while all this foreplay is great, says Mark, there is nothing that quite connects you more than being inside a woman. To me, there is nothing more intimate than vaginal penetration. Not even anal intercourse."

His big complaint, however, is that women don't pull their weight in this department. "As much as guys have to learn to thrust properly, and position himself to rub against her clitoris, women have to learn how to grind and use their vaginal muscles. A lot of women just spread their hips and their lips and enjoy the ride. They don't control things enough during intercourse."

Another real turn-on during intercourse, according to Nathan, is lots of eye contact. "Communicating with her eyes is great. When her eyes say, 'I am doing this to you and I am really enjoying it.' A woman who's good at this does run the risk of ending the evening's activities early, but oh, it's good."

Mark is very reflective about intercourse. In fact, doing it on top of a mirror is right up there as one of his big turn-ons. "It's a great way to become at ease with your bodies and to really see and subsequently feel what's going on."

You can't escape a discussion of what turns guys' cranks without the infamous two-on-one scenario.

"Like skydiving, being with two women is something you want to do before you die," laughs John.

Geronimo!

How to Score

What Turns a Woman On

"WE HAD THIS amazing sex in my room, and after, I went downstairs. When I came back up a while later to see what he was doing, he had cleaned my entire bedroom!" my friend tells me excitedly over the phone. Granted this was only three-week-old lust talking, but—as someone whose own room often lives up to the name of this column—I was impressed by the gesture. "It was such a selfless act," she continued. "It let me know this person really wants to do things for me. It was very sweet and a real turn-on."

What makes a good lover a great lover is highly subjective, of course. But after talking to several women aged 20 to 35, one thing is clear: while good motor skills don't go unnoticed, often it has more to do with what he does when you're *not* in bed together.

"One time I was on the phone in the kitchen and he dropped to his knees and started kissing my legs," Christine (all names changed so no one tries to steal their marvellous men) tells me— a shit-eating grin on her face. "When I looked down, he started laughing and said 'Sorry but your legs are just *so-o-o-o* sexy.'"

The best thing about it, she adds, is that he didn't necessarily do it with the intention of leading to sex. "I could tell he just did it for the pleasure of touching my body and making me feel good."

"Sometimes when we're walking down the street he turns to me and tells me how hot I am and how much he wants me," says Shelly, with her beau for over a year. "It's really reassuring because he's very attractive and women and men hit on him all the time."

Flattery will get you everywhere, guys. "He tells me I'm beautiful, smart and well spoken all the time," says Brenda, who's in her first long-term relationship since her marriage broke up a couple years back. "He helps me see myself as a sexual, sensual person, and it makes me want to act on that."

But buttering us up doesn't just cater to women's narcissistic tendencies. Sometimes it's necessary to deal with the baggage about their bodies which so many women lug into the sack with them. "I have all these things about my body that I worry about, like if I have too much sex I get bladder infections," explains Elaine, who's about to marry a guy she met overseas nine months ago. "He's very good about it. He'll say, 'Okay dear, you better have a glass of water. Now shut up and have some fun.' It's very funny and makes me relax."

Having a partner who can relax you is definitely up there on the "how to make a woman feel good" list.

"I'm really self-conscious about my legs and thighs," admits Shelly. "He spends a long time massaging them and telling me how much he loves them and how beautiful I am. Massage is really important. Especially if it's done without sex as a goal." That's twice now.

"Sometimes a guy wants you to get off more than *you* do," complains Brenda. "But if I'm in a space where I can't come—like when I have a lot on my mind or whatever—it's just not gonna happen. So, instead of doing that ego thing where he must make me come, my guy just tries to pleasure me as much as possible. If it doesn't result in a big bang, it's no big deal, as long as I'm enjoying it."

It also helps that he's learned a little trick that works every time when she does want to get off. "He focuses on my clitoris, and sucks it in and out very fast." Brenda explains. "It works every time. Now, because he's found this thing, he knows that he can get me off pretty much at any time. It gives us the luxury of exploring other things and then, if I get grumpy and really want to get off, he just has to do this little trick." I did say good motor skills don't go *entirely* unappreciated.

As far as technique goes, Lisa says her lover's strength is that he's very intuitive. "He never does anything for a really long time," she explains. "Like if he's going down on me, he often changes the pressure, direction and style."

And the area he's exploring, adds Christine. "He moves around my whole body and doesn't immediately go for 'the zone.' He lets the momentum build and gives me time to become really aroused."

"Yeah, so many guys still learn 'first base = kiss; second base-touch breasts," echoes Elaine.

And lighten up, guys. "We just play," says Brenda. "He doesn't hurry through anything to get to penetration. In fact, he's probably less penetration-oriented than I am. On occasion, I've had to coax him into it."

Sometimes we need a little coaxing ourselves. Elaine said she found she became uptight about oral sex after she had an abortion. "I told my current lover that once, and now he always spends a lot of time relaxing me, massaging the area, and talking me very sweetly into oral sex."

The first time Samantha's boyfriend wanted to go down on her they were camping. This made her nervous because she's a clean-freak and likes to shower before she lets anyone down there. "But he asked me if he could taste me, like he was seeking permission, checking first to see if I was okay with it. I really appreciated it." Samantha admits she still prefers to wash beforehand. "So now, if one of us suggests a shower, it's a sign," she laughs.

Keeping things clean is not always desirable when it comes to oral skills however. "Sometimes he'll talk to me in a loving, tender way during sex," says Christine. "But sometimes it's aggressive and raunchy."

Lisa admits that while talking dirty is a turn-on for her, often she finds it difficult to overcome the discomfort and shyness. "Sometimes we'll get off on simply boosting each other's self-esteem. I think it's really sexual to say things like 'you're beautiful; I love your body; you're such a nice person; I really loved that you did that for me today'—anything to make the person feel good."

Another hot way to communicate in bed is to simply look at

each other, she adds. "I find eye contact very powerful and a real turn-on. At times it's so intense it can even be even harder to do than talking to each other in bed."

Communicating via eye contact doesn't just work wonders during sex. "If we're out at a party, he'll slide me a sly look full of innuendo," says Brenda. "We flirt a lot and it's really playful. And it doesn't always lead to falling into bed, which makes it feel more genuine. A lot of guys abandon that once they're secure in the relationship. We still interact with each other like we're new lovers." Now that's a goal everyone should strive for.

States of Desire
Doing the Labido Lambada

DEAR JOSEY,

I have a problem. Well, at least my boyfriend of nine months thinks so. Our first argument was that he always makes the first moves when it comes to sex and I didn't make him feel as if I want him. I never really get the chance to do the "starting." I get home from work, we eat, then the next thing I know his hands are all over me… every day it's the same. Shouldn't I get the chance to relax a few moments and at least try to feel a little sexy before throwing myself into passion?

Don't get me wrong, I love sex with him. But he was used to these "Give it to me, give it to me, ooohhh Baby, let me swallow your load…" kind of women. I'm just not like that. Although I'd sometimes like to be, I'm just not able to pull off the Porn Queen act. I think the problem is one part lack of imagination and two parts low self-esteem.

The point is that I don't want to fake wanting it or him. I'm not expecting to find some miracle "cure" that will put me on overdrive 24 hours a day either. I want to be sexy in a way that won't repulse me or make me feel inadequate. I want to be sexy in a way that will bring him to his knees. I want to find a happy middle. Do you know if such a thing exists?

Looking-for-the-middle

* * *

Dear Looking-for-the-middle,

Perhaps you could start by having the phrase, "quality not quantity" tattooed on your boyfriend's wild willy. You gotta wonder how much *he* can be really enjoying all the sex you're not into. In fact, after the tattoo, maybe he might want to invest in one of those blow-up dolls, 'cause that's all he seems to be using you for, a live masturbatory machine. Ask him if he knows the difference between making love to you or with you. I've always found it to be a lot more fun with both partners present.

As for becoming a "Baby, give it to me, I wanna swallow your load" Porn Queen, please. If that's his idea of a woman really enjoying herself and getting into sex, revoke his XXX-video membership immediately. And do you honestly think your self-esteem is gauged by the intensity of your desire to "swallow his load?"

Now, tsk, tsking out of the way, lopsided libidos is probably one of the most common complaints in long-term relationships. Once you're past the initial stages where seeing your partner butter his toast is enough to turn you on, things get familiar and desire starts to feel like work. Pretty soon, you develop a very complex communication system around it. He touches you, you shrug him off, he rolls over. End of conversation. At least that's the stereotype.

He wants sex more than she does and she never takes the initiative. Then he stops taking the initiative, because she's never into it, then you both lie there staring at the ceiling wondering what happened to all that good sex you used to have. Then you have affairs.

So what's the deal? Is it simply true that men just want it more? Anytime, anywhere, right? I suppose if I was told that all my life, I'd start to believe it too. Unfortunately, as a woman, I was raised to believe exactly the opposite message about myself. I'm not supposed to really want it, I'm a good girl. Sex is for making babies.

As a result, I think, for a lot of women, turning down sex often feels more natural than initiating it, whereas for a guy to turn down sex makes him feel like a freak. What would his buddies think? "She was all over me, but I didn't feel like it." Better to have mediocre sex than none at all, whereas, for her, maybe she'd rather hold off and have great sex, even if that means having it less often.

As for his complaint that you don't initiate and it makes him feel like you don't want him, try turning the tables. Say, just say, your boyfriend did give you "a few moments to at least try to feel a little sexy," then responded to your advances with, "Sorry, I'm tired, I'm not into it tonight." I'm sure you'd be hurt, probably even more so because guys are supposed to want it all the time. If he's not into it, it's hard not to feel like the Bride of Frankenstein. Ever gotten into it hot and heavy, only to find his less-than-enthusiastic desire greets your touch? Kinda knocks the old ego around. Saying no to sex without hurting the other person's feelings is sensitive work.

That's because desire develops in our minds where it gets messed up with all the other stuff going on up there—egos, sexual histories, memories, stress, what's on TV... By the time desire makes its way through all that stuff and gets to your crotch, he's probably already in over his head (yeah, that one). Whoa doggy! Since you weren't ready when he got there, your immediate reaction is to turn off. Egos have a tendency to jump to conclusions, and suddenly this resistance is about rejection of him, rather than a perhaps less than crystal clear request from you for an alternative approach (showering you with affection with no strings attached doesn't hurt), a bit more patience (at least enough time to drum up a fantasy or two if need be), or, if necessary, a raincheck.

Your boyfriend may have a stronger sex drive than you (though I suspect it's more out of habit than real desire) but it's never gonna be much fun for him if he doesn't allow you to get in touch with the ups and downs of yours. And, trust me, nothing brings a guy to his knees more than a woman who is in tune with her sexual desires.

You're ultimately responsible for your own pleasure, but he can certainly take the pressure off so you feel safe enough to give yourself permission to take it. Desire on command does not exist (unless that's part of the fun) and the only middle you will find if you start taking the initiative out of guilt rather than real desire will be the middle-of-the-road.

Location, Location...

Where's the Weirdest Place You've Had Sex?

"WHAT SECTION?"

"Drama."

"C'mon, you can't get away with having sex in a Blockbuster Video store."

"It wasn't busy. We were quick."

At least it wasn't the family section. The best I've done was the parking garage of a building under construction on a hot summer day in broad daylight.

Oh, and I once gave a guy a blowjob on a bus.

Yes, folks—it's the most FAQ in Truth or Dare: Where's the weirdest place you've had sex?

A one-up on the bus blowjob: "A friend of mine did it in the bathroom of a Voyageur bus."

I'm impressed. It's hard enough to pee in one of those things.

It's odd how so many people can't come up with their own "weird-location sex stories" but always seem to have plenty of tales about "friends." "The great thing about telling your friends' stories is that you can elaborate on them and live your own fantasies through them," was one particularly creative explanation for this phenomenon.

"Friends of mine did it in a church bell tower in Holland," relates one guy. To be fair, he did go on to share his own overseas religious experience.

"We did it in a monastery in Italy." He and his girlfriend got separated from the group and decided to take full advantage of the time alone. It was obvious what they'd been up to when they hooked up with the group again sporting their post-sex-in-a-monastery hairdos. Not all of us can be led into temptation, though. "We chickened out in a church," another guy recounts.

It's not just getting caught by God that makes it exciting. The possibility of getting caught by *anyone* seems to be exciting enough to place sex in public places on top of so many people's sex-in-weird-places list.

"We did it in the law-school library."

"In a bank machine." I'm sure they weren't actually in the bank machine but you know what he means. I guess you might say they were making, groan... deposits and withdrawals.

"Onstage, before a play." Hey, part of the set included a futon. What are you gonna do? It would have gone over without a hitch except one of the actors found the used condom wrapper.

Next on the list is the not-so-public but still tantalizingly risky locations.

"In the office after work. We started playing computer games and one thing led to another."

"In the laundry room of an apartment building. This woman invited me to come over for a swim in the rooftop pool of her friend's apartment building. I got there and there was no pool."

And the laundry room is the next obvious choice, of course.

"In our apartment with my parents in the next room." That's almost as scary as God.

Having sex in less-than-private situations isn't just about the excitement of getting caught. The location itself can be very invigorating. Sex in the great outdoors, for example.

Whether it's a little side street in the city, as it was for one outdoorsy couple, or the dewy green of the 18th hole of a golf course at dusk.

"I was the 19th hole," laughs the woman of this adventurous duo.

"Snowshoeing at 30 below." I find that even harder to believe than Blockbuster.

The woods is a popular one among the boys, my little survey revealed. "There's nothing like a blowjob in the woods, lying back looking up at the sky and the trees." Brings out the Grizzly Adams in them, I suppose.

"Under a bridge with a train going over and rapids nearby—that was awesome," a lesbian friend tells me. "It was also the last guy I ever slept with."

After that, why bother, really?

"In a park at night."

"Did you get naked?"

"Yeah, we had our bathing suits on so it made it easy."

That's something to consider— sex in less conventional locales can really test your coordination skills. "Doggie style in a rowboat—that was a challenge." "In a train bathroom en route from Paris to Amsterdam." More exotic, but the bus bathroom would still be tougher.

"Bareback on a horse." Right. Danger can also be part of the excitement. "Anal sex on the edge of a cliff," for example, somehow makes perfect sense.

Mind-altering drugs also seem to inspire people to have sex in the darndest places.

"In a waterfall on mushrooms."

"Inside a big plastic orange tube in a children's playground on acid. We couldn't tell if we were getting off or not. It was very weird." No doubt. That's the thing about sex under unusual circumstances. Often fantasy is better than fiction.

"We climbed up on the roof, thinking it would be very romantic. But we got up there and the roof was covered in gravel so we tried to do it on this slanted part that didn't have gravel and kept sliding down. It wasn't quite the spontaneous excitement we were hoping for." For another woman, the welts left by the rocks from doing it under a bridge are more memorable than the sex.

Sex on the beach is another one like that. You end up picking sand outta yer butt for days. Or soothing the crab bites on it, as was the case for one guy.

Also, because men's parts are more accessible and quicker to arouse, they get to enjoy full benefits from the event more often than she does. Predictably, for example, the little scene in the video store didn't include a climax—for her.

For some reason, several people I spoke to apologized for not having any really great weird-location sex stories to tell. I think we have this notion that wilder and weirder means better when it comes to sex, and if you haven't done it hang gliding, you're sexually repressed. But you gotta wonder when you're lying there with a ladder in your back on some guy's antique firetruck in his barn, as one woman retells, if the whole thing might not be more about him trying to impress her with his hoses.

"It's not where you're doing it but what you're doing," was a sober thought offered by one guy. "And no matter where you are, it's the connection between you that makes it exciting."

Granted, when you're at the animal-lust early stages of a relationship, it seems natural to suddenly find yourself doing it in the aisle of the city bus.

If you've been together for a while, sometimes you simply need a change of scenery from the bedroom. If you think about it, though—with a little redecorating (light a candle or two, throw on some fancy sheets, maybe toss a bit of gravel in your bed), your bedroom could become a whole new weird place to have sex.

Sex Unlimited

Bringing Fantasy to Life

UNDOUBTEDLY, our minds are our most active sex organ. But surprisingly—despite all the thought we give to the matter—most of us apply very little of this personal sex research to real life. Which is fine. Some fantasies are better left in your head (especially ones involving small furry animals and/or family members). But sometimes you want to let your thoughts spill over into real life; act out a fantasy or two, push your sexual limits, experiment. Testing these waters with a lover can be exhilarating, hilarious, and very hot. It can also be terrifying. Which is why so many of us never get around to it.

What if she's not into it? What if I make a fool of myself? How do you broach the subject? What if he thinks I'm a pervert?

Getting over this with someone new is bad enough. Getting over it with someone you've been with for years can be brutal. Old habits die hard.

That's why I think it's a really good idea to check things out early. Find out what each other is into. Long car rides are good for this, as are walks in the park, beach, in the country, what have you—any neutral, relaxed environment that allows you to ask questions, swap fantasies, and reveal inhibitions without fearing you'll be laughed out of bed. It's best to be somewhere quasi-private as well, in case you suddenly feel inspired to act out the discussion. Unless, of course, public sex is one of your fantasies.

Talking about your fantasies is good 'cause it's safe (you don't have to act on it) and informative (even if you don't act on it, you find out what turns them on and off). Verbalizing your sexual imagination can also be a real turn-on.

In fact, talking dirty seems a common initiator for a more adventurous sex life. A chatty friend of mine said she opened the floodgates about six weeks into her current relationship by talking sexy in bed. "Now he talks about what things feel like, about what he'd like to do, about how beautiful and sexy I am, or about specific parts of my body," she says, the smirk on her face telling the whole story. "Sometimes it's in a loving, tender way; sometimes it's very sexual—real aggressive and raunchy. I love that, and I love talking like that too."

If you're not ready for a full-out tongue-lashing, you might want to replay some of your sexier moments together—like how you remember when you were both in the shower all slippery and wet and you went down on him. As you get more and more comfy, you can be more and more direct and explicit. Fun, fun, fun.

Respect and trust are biggies when it comes to exploring the outer limits. I always find it a bit jarring when someone is into really intense stuff right off the bat. As one friend said to me, "How relaxed are you going to be with someone who throws you around their apartment on your first date?"

I tend to agree. If I'm gonna let someone spank me, tie me up, or play nurse to me, I want to at least know if I can stand being around them. Mostly I want to be sure I can trust them. "I can see our sex getting more adventurous because there is complete trust," my smirking friend continues. "I feel like this is our territory and there's no one else in it (unless we invite them). It's safe and we can explore whatever we want."

Certainly part of what makes daring sexual experiences so intense is relinquishing some of your self-control. Giving yourself to someone in that way—putting yourself at their mercy—can make you feel very exposed. If you're with someone you trust, this can be an incredibly powerful, loving feeling. At worst, it can be a weird power-trip. Then again, exploring the power dynamics of a relationship through sexual play is another great way to get to know someone.

And develop intimacy. Nothing like a nice golden shower to bring two people together. Intimacy goes a long way toward keeping the passion meter ticking in a long-term relationship.

But paradoxically, while the familiarity and comfort of a long-term relationship should make it easy to explore new things, more often than not, if you've never talked about it, routine and complacency set in. Eventually, the lines of communication are too difficult to open and we fall into the monogamy-equals-monotony rut.

Communication is the key when venturing into uncharted

territory. You have to know that you can say no if something makes you uncomfortable, or that you can laugh if something makes you feel ridiculous. Because face it, sometimes reality just doesn't live up to fantasy, and while wearing diapers and being treated like a baby seem like a turn-on in your mind, you might find yourself less than ga-ga about the real thing. The thought of being in a threesome may excite you, but the reality of it might be threatening or make you feel silly or scared.

That's because fantasy is emotionally loaded. Acting on it may trigger unexpected reactions, both positive and negative. You both have to be prepared for whatever comes up—be it stuff from your childhood, or crusty old moral dilemmas about what's good and bad or "dirty."

In fact, when you're playing on a psychological level, such as with power games, role playing, dominance, submission, bondage, etc., the emotional often overrides the physical. But that's what makes it so fun, too.

Coming Clean
Learning Your Partner's STDs

So, THIS FRIEND of mine goes to the doctor, right—a routine check-up. There she is, lying back spread-eagled on the comfy paper bedspread, feet elegantly propped in the stirrups, staring up into the fluorescent lights, cranked open with a speculum. The doctor's up to her elbows inside, prodding and poking—"ovary, yup, feels fine; other one, yup, fine too; uterus, still there…" and so on. I—uh, I mean my friend—casually wonders out loud about a couple of strange bumps she's recently encountered "down there" (never you mind what she was doing feeling around down there). The doctor looks up from her exploratory mission and asks my friend to show her the bumps. "Condyloma," the doctor says nonchalantly. Condawhat? "Warts, venereal warts."

Oh great, thinks my friend (we're very close—she tells me everything.) Uh, how exactly do you get them? she asks, even though her mind has already raced well beyond that to, "That fucker—who did he sleep with," because she knows she's been a little angel for months now. "There has to be direct sexual contact," the doctor answers. "But don't worry, they're very common, and easy to treat." Yeah, whatever, lady. My friend's thinking has already moved onto: I bet you it was her, even though he told me nothing happened between them. Man, he's toast! "But it's a virus," the doctor continues somewhere in the background of her runaway mind. "It can be dormant in your system for years and then the warts suddenly show up, sometimes due to stress. I even heard one story where a doctor diagnosed venereal warts on an 85-year-old nun who swore she'd hadn't had sex since her teenage years." Huh? I—damn, I mean, my friend—snaps out of her jealous rage, and suddenly her Catholic-school conditioning takes over. Nuns don't lie, she thinks. Oh no, that means… she probably got it from some jerk she slept with ages ago.

Probably that lousy one-night stand she met in Cleveland. Or the tree planter—living out in the woods with all those hippies, everyone sleeping with each other—yeah, I bet it was him, she thinks.

And if she didn't get warts from her boyfriend, she's gonna have to try and explain how she got them and make him poke around to see if he's the lucky winner of a brand-new STD. Groan, he'll love that. He's even more ignorant than she is about this stuff. He's sure to jump to all kinds of unsavoury conclusions—Toad Girl's been having sex in sewers or licking toilet seats again, he'll imagine. On top of all this, said Toad Girl is gonna have to let someone take a torch to her privates and blast the nasty little buggers off.

STDs are so much fun. Never mind the stress and anxiety

they cause as a health problem, almost worse is the stigma. You know the attitude. Someone—especially a lover—tells you he's got herpes, and, instead of thanking him for letting you know, you think, eeww! and can't help but wonder about where he's been. So, because having an STD tends to make you feel less than pristine, people avoid telling their lovers altogether. Better to risk it than confront a new lover with a list of what they might want to protect themselves from if they sleep with little-ole diseased you, right?

The shame can even stop some people from getting checked out at all. (As can the mention of the word "swab," hey boys?) Others don't bother to get checked out because they don't want to have to deal with prejudice or uncomfortable questions. One guy I know swears that when he was nineteen his doctor gave him a double slathering of a painful treatment for venereal warts on his bum after he answered yes when the doctor asked if he was a homosexual.

Sometimes STDs are tough to talk about because you have to tell your partner you've slept with someone else. As if, by not telling, the other person won't be infected. Nice logic.

Another friend of mine found out the hard way. She moved to a new city, in part to escape a bad relationship. One day at work, she went to the bathroom to relieve an incessant itch and ended up scratching a little critter out of her pubes. She had crabs. When she saw the guy years later, she thanked him for the lovely going-away present. "He said, 'Oh you mean chlamydia.' I couldn't believe it. Two for the price of one," my astounded friend tells me. "And worse he tells me that his new girlfriend got chlamydia from him too and told everyone it came from me."

Ah, the source—always good for a little finger pointing, shame, guilt and embarrassment. Of course, it's always the other person's fault.

Another friend got crabs in Greece from a guy she was living with. "I only spoke a bit of Greek, and he only spoke a little English, so when I asked him where he got crabs, he conveniently came back with, 'I no understand.'"

And try tracking down Kwellada lotion in Greece. It's bad enough here having to plunk down a can of the shit on the counter at your local pharmacy ("Could I have a price check on the Kwellada? Toad Girl's apparently got crabs too!"). "And have you seen the size of the roaches in Greece?" she goes on. "You have to smash them with a brick. I felt so gross. I had visions of the crabs growing to cockroach size."

Of course, people come up with all kinds of stories about how they got infected (I was playing with my friend's goldfish, and, uh...), leaving most people completely misinformed about how you really do put yourself at risk for different STDs.

STDs are scary and stressful enough. And viruses like venereal warts and Herpes are your friends for life. Pretending you don't have them and not enlightening the people you have sex with to save yourself a little embarrassment is pretty selfish. And if your partner goes "eeww!" you might want to consider what you're doing with the lunkhead. Besides, did you know it is illegal to knowingly transmit a venereal disease? And if a person refuses treatment once diagnosed, they can be forced into it by law. But the swab, the boys cry. Hey, try having a nice, cold, metal speculum wrenched open inside you.

Condom Nation

How Come We're Still Not Protecting Ourselves?

I'M NOT SURE if y'all are aware of this, but unprotected sex can kill you. AIDS has been with us for well over a decade, yet most surveys still show only about 25 percent of the population in Canada using condoms.

Most surveys also report that only about 15 percent of the population say catching or spreading HIV was even a concern during sex. Hello?! That's one serious case of denial. Not surprisingly, these figures rise significantly among gay men. About 75 percent of the gay population regularly use condoms.

This, of course, can be attributed to the fact that gay men were getting tired of watching all their friends die so they organized, fought for and created effective safe-sex campaigns targeting their own community. The heterosexual community still hasn't got its shit together. Our federal government has never even done a national publicity campaign promoting safe sex. How much effort would it be to maybe slip a free condom into our census package? And many schools still aren't comfortable letting health educators in to talk about safe sex. It's time to get a collective grip.

◆◆◆ *Josey Vogels*

Hey, I'm just as pissed as you that our little window of sexual freedom between the pill and AIDS has been shut. It was great while it lasted. You have to admit, there's nothing quite like intercourse without a condom. Which is no doubt why a lot of us are still doing it. But I don't think simply giving in to what feels good is the only reason we are having so much latex-free sex.

There are other reasons we aren't having safe sex. Fear, for one—fears that are bigger, more tangible than AIDS—like the fear of losing your woody.

I know for a fact that some guys lose their erection when they put a condom on. Call me crazy, but I've heard men can have more than one. Still, it seems the anxiety is too much for some men. Before you know it, just the crinkling sound of a condom wrapper is enough to leave him limp. I'm told some guys actually refuse to wear one to avoid the embarrassment. Unfortunately, some women don't refuse to have sex with them.

There are lots of other reasons why we take the risk. Sometimes, if you slip once with a lover, it's easier to slip again. Even if you do manage—in the heat of the moment—to lunge over to the bedside drawer without injury and seductively tear open a condom with your teeth, whip it out, slide it on, and lube it without missing a beat, now suddenly you're committed to intercourse. Going down on it is about as fun as sucking on your Tupperware. Guess we gotta stick it in—and keep it there. Boring. It's much more tempting to just go with the flow and let things unfold according to your desires. And to learn to live with the guilt. Trust me, I'm Catholic—you can learn to live with guilt.

So what's it gonna take? Will a few more posters change our behaviour?

"All we can do is keep hammering the message home," says the public relations manager of Durex, a condom manufacturer who regularly conducts surveys about Canadians sexual habits. "Obviously, Canadians are not getting enough messages about protecting themselves when having casual sex."

But, as gay groups have been saying for years, the message has to be tailored to the group at which it's aimed. The folks who make condoms agree. "We've found the younger generation doesn't listen to gloom and doom messages about AIDS and safe sex," they say. "We take a much more humorous approach."

They've also tried to improve the image of the condom, to help people see it as a good thing, not an necessary evil. "We've come up with softer, subtler ads in an attempt to inject some romance into condom use."

As far as I'm concerned, what's more romantic than wanting your lover to be safe?

Modern Love

Sexposition
A Trip to the Salon Érotique

THE SOFT-SPOKEN, silver-haired gentleman in the booth was very matter-of-fact as he extolled the features of a fancy, new vibrator. It looked like a flesh-coloured softie ice-cream cone with ridge after ridge of pleasure-promising rubber. It was more flexible than most models I've tried. Unfortunately, there were no free samples.

We were at Le Salon Érotique, Montreal's first annual sex trade show. We've got car shows, boat shows and home shows; why not sex?

The floor show was impressive. Twenty-five display booths offered everything from the latest in herbal aphrodisiacs to phone-sex line start-up kits.

"It's the first time all the people working in this business have been able to get together and meet each other," the organizer is telling me enthusiastically while we tour the Pussycat Lounge booth. I'm trying to share her excitement but the cunning linguistics going on the screen in the velvet-draped, softly lit space are presenting stiff competition.

Well, it's about time these folks finally started networking. Of course, no trade show would be complete without some live demonstrations for the public.

The, uh, lingerie show would have made Uncle Sam proud. Miss America came out clad in Stars and Stripes and proceeded to demonstrate the effectiveness of a little audience participation in getting folks interested in what you've got to offer. I'm sure the lucky fella's date was thrilled.

The big treat for us girls—aside from the guy in the "cock" underwear with the strategically placed rooster head and the guy in the elephant trunks—was the live Chippendales show.

"The Canadian Chippendales Chapter is our biggest attraction," the organizer assures me. I chatted with dancer Maurice (though it's hard to tell them apart), who's been with Chippendales for four years. He loves his job (you get to wear those nifty white collars and bow ties) even if his girlfriend has a rough time with it once in awhile. "We're like a hockey team," he tells me. (I guess that explains the haircuts.) "We tour around, they put us up in hotels, we train three times a week, we're all in it together." These guys are way more wholesome than hockey players; they can't drink or do drugs, and they have to keep their peckers in their pants. They'd make any mom proud.

After all that girl fun, I met up with my friend back at one of several sex-shop display booths. He was the one wearing the baseball cap topped with a huge rubber penis head. We "networked" our way to the next booth, one of Canada's top gay-porn video distributors.

"Weird sells these days," the guy informed me when I asked

what the current big sellers were amongst his heterosexual titles. For example, he told me, one of his hottest new titles is Ready to Drop, a porn video featuring pregnant women who are, well, ready to drop. I guess family values really are making a comeback.

Ninety-five percent of all porn videos in Canada come from the U.S., the sales guy informed us. In an attempt to redress this, he and his partner have recently embarked on some of their own productions.

One of these, Mind Sex, he proudly boasts, is their response to the current increase in the number of women demanding porn videos. (Always looking out for our interests, these guys.) "What'd you do different?" I ask. "This one's got a story, it's full of emotion," he's practically bursting with it himself. "There are scenes in this video, let me tell ya, they'll make you cry." When I pointed out that tears are not exactly what I'm after when it comes to porn, he handed me a free copy to check out. When I watched it later, it did make me cry, only it was from laughing so hard at the utterly horrific acting and pathetic story line.

After being told on several occasions how much we women like emotions and story lines when it comes to sex, it was refreshing to come across Les Éditions Beaulimar, a Montreal-based distribution house owned by Mariette Beaulieu. She's been in the business for almost ten years and says, "Yeah, women like stories, but women want hardcore stuff too. They just want it done with taste, that's the difference." That's why she specializes in European titles which she says are much higher quality than American porn.

Next door to Beaulieu's booth was a company that specializes in lingerie home shows. Kinda like Tupperware parties, except they're demonstrating crotchless panties instead of plastic bowls.

The final booth we came across was an erotic portrait service. Could make for some pretty interesting "personalized" Christmas cards this year, I thought.

Even the home show couldn't come up with a holiday gift idea that good.

Psychic Alliance
Turning Your Love Life Over to the Stars

"HELLO JOSEY," the voice answered the phone. "Wow, you are psychic." I was impressed. After all, I hadn't specified when I would call. "I've got call display," confessed Gilles, a phone operator for the Psychic Network of Love.

Men are not the only suckers when it comes to 1-900-FORK-OVER ads. But while they're calling 1-900-HOT-BABE to cope, women, being more cerebral of course, call psychics. Back pages of adult, that is men's, magazines lure the boys with butts and boobs, but women's mags lure us with scads of ads promising the answers to all our love and relationship problems just a phone call away.

Gilles told me I was like a barge when it came to relationships. I carry way too much cargo and can't pick up speed. I would do better as a speedboat. Then I could set a goal, rev up my motor and zip through torrential waters like no tomorrow. Anyone in my way, watch out. "But," he cautioned, "be careful you don't overturn all the canoes and paddle boats along the way with your waves." The trick is to "respect the ecology around your goals," Gilles told me. I liked that.

They're big on metaphors, these psychics. Later in the call, Gilles described me as a female lion, purring one minute, claws out the next. I like to play rough, he told me, and he described a vision he had of me swinging male cubs around, "not to be mean," he said, "that's just the way you have to play to survive in this world." I am lion, hear me roar!

Marilyn, of the Latoya Jackson Psychic Network, sounded tired. It took her a while to cosmically connect, even with my name, birth date, and all that psychic energy I was sending over the phone line to go on. In between drags off her cig (one advantage to being a phone psychic), she flipped Tarot cards and gave me the lowdown on the future of my current relationship. Apparently, it didn't have one. "It's already over," she told me. "Wait a minute, based on what?" I asked, a bit taken aback.

"The Tower card was the first card I turned up and it indicates that something is over." I had just finished my lunch, I suggested. "It's going to go one way or the other," she continued. What amazing insight, I thought to myself. "You have self-will, you are not a victim and you are ultimately responsible for your own future." So, what? I'm paying you $50 to tell me I shouldn't even be asking you?

"That's the problem," Marilyn explained. "A lot of people don't realize this and they call a psychic wanting to know their future but it's not there, it's something you're creating every day. You have free will and not even God's gonna interfere with that. Of course, the scary part is that the responsibility is yours as to what you do because only you can affect your future."

That's why I want someone to tell me what to do, Marilyn. This Tower Card explosion thing bothered me, but our 10-minute phone company-imposed maximum was up. I needed more.

I called The Love Tarot and spoke to Marie. She was good. Marie described my relationship to a Tee. It was a bit unnerving. She too thought I should ditch him. "Tell him you love him, tell him you'll even leave a trail of bread crumbs to let him know where you've gone if he wants to find you, but rediscover your power," was her other-worldly advice. "You've lost sight of your strength and let me tell you, honey, I just turned up the Priestess card which says you are one powerful mama."

Flattery will get you everywhere, Marie. It might even get you another call from me sometime, I thought to myself. I liked this woman. In true psychic fashion, Marie read my mind. "I just got the 60-second beep that our 10-minute maximum is up, honey, but my name's Marie and my extension is 300, I'm on Sunday to Thursday so if you need to cuss and discuss, give me a holler and we can chat."

Ah, so that's how they get you. There may be a ten-minute maximum per call but you can call as many times as you like. And people do. To the tune of $120 million in the US alone last year. And those are only the ones who pay. By the sound of Marie's "Please be nice and pay up or I starve" spiel at the beginning of our call, many don't.

So why are people shelling out all this dough to have a total stranger sort out their life? Gilles says he often feels more like a therapist than a psychic. "I'm a friendly ear," he says. "In the old days, people went to their priest or the guy at the general store with their problems. Now the priest only keeps office hours on Tuesdays from 4 to 7 and you don't want to discuss your husband's drinking with the guy with the funny green hair who works down at the corner store."

Fast-food therapy without the "seeing a therapist" stigma.

As for there being some cosmic force influencing this advice, I don't know. I have to say, the accuracy about what was going on in my life was a bit creepy. But then again, there is enough common human experience that if you're good at it you can speak generally enough to make it specific to anyone's life, even with the smallest amount of detail from them. A revelation that you're unhappy in your job might inspire a statement like "you have burning desires and aspirations." Pretty safe, unless you prefer to think of yourself as a lazy slug who will never amount to anything.

In the end, the combination of an objective observer telling you exactly what you (along with all your friends) have been telling yourself all along, and surmising enough detail to make you believe there is some greater power at work, might push you to take action.

And keep you coming back for more.

Power Trip
Life as a Professional Dominatrix

As a professional dominatrix, she's usually the one with the handcuffs and the control. But even Domina Sylvia couldn't contend with the boys in blue when five members of the morality squad broke into her Montreal apartment and arrested her for running, keeping and living in a common bawdy house.

It's charming, don't you think? A common bawdy house. It conjures up images of buxom lasses doing the can-can, their heaving bosoms beckoning, leaving unsuspecting men powerless to their wanton ways.

The definition in the Criminal Code is not nearly so exciting—or specific. It describes a common bawdy house as a place where "prostitution or indecent acts" take place. "A whorehouse" is how Domina Sylvia's uninvited guests described it.

Problem is, Sylvia Wahl doesn't consider herself a whore. Not that there's anything wrong with being a whore, but whores exchange sex for money. As a dominatrix, Wahl never lets her slaves get that far with her.

"What I do is domination," says Wahl, whose German accent and sculpted features give her that perfect mistress edge. "There is no masturbation or sexual release on either side."

This is part of the Dominatrix Code of Honour, Wahl stresses; violating it would damage her reputation as a professional.

Another rule is to play it safe and respect limits. I witnessed this first-hand at a demo Wahl did as part of a fetish convention (they got 'em for everything these days). About twenty of us huddled around a raised platform in Wahl's dungeon (a custom-designed double room in her apartment that looks rather like a macabre McDonald's playground) while she demonstrated the art of domin-ation. Safety came up over and over, whether it was showing us how to whip someone's back without giving them permanent kidney damage or establishing code words between slave and master to know when no means no. For example, if she thinks she might like to punish someone with a golden shower, she'll suss out her slave's feelings about it first. "I'll threaten to pee on him if he doesn't behave," she explained at the time. "If he begs for mercy, I don't proceed, but if he says, 'anything you say, mistress,' that's a green light."

She also takes safety precautions for herself. If she's alone in her dungeon with one slave, she'll have another one in the kitchen doing the dishes in case anything goes wrong.

Wahl learned the, uh, ropes back home in Germany about six years ago as an apprentice to a veteran mistress. Somehow her work as a court-house secretary began to seem dull, and she got into the domination biz full-time. She loves her work. "It's a power trip," she admits. "I get pleasure out of teasing, torturing and humiliating them. I like the challenge; it's fun trying new things, different equipment, pushing limits. It's more about control than sex. And it's always consensual—they like it and I like it." And, she adds, while she also enjoys exploring S&M games in her personal life, she makes a rule of never sleeping with her clients. Don't we all aspire to making a living doing something we love? But it's not always about money either, says Wahl.

Lots of her "clients" like to drop by the house just to bring her gifts, clean the floors, or take her shopping. "It's very convenient, really," she laughs. "These guys would do anything for me just to see me for a few moments."

So if being a dominatrix isn't exactly prostitution, is it at least indecent? Although the view up her slave's butt while he crawled around in a leather jock strap and licked her boots during the demo wasn't exactly savoury, I wouldn't call it indecent. As far as I could tell, it was a fully understood and mutually acceptable relationship between two adults. That's more than I could say for a lot of "normal" relationships I've seen. Face it, indecency is a subjective term. Which makes the Criminal Code definition of a bawdy house ridiculous. When I asked the morality squad how the term "indecency" was defined, they simply said it was up to the judge in each case to interpret. Great. Unless he's one of her clients, what are the chances he'll understand?

For Wahl, what's indecent is asking people to repress their sexual desires and fantasies. For most of her clients, says Wahl, her dungeon is the one place they can safely live out their fantasies. "If they couldn't come here, they would be depressed or they might act out their frustration in less healthy ways."

As for the charge that she is exploiting what many would consider to be "unhealthy" sexual attitudes, her logic runs something along the lines of "hey, people shouldn't eat junk food either but they still sell loads of it." And besides, have you priced torture equipment lately? While rates are confidential, Wahl assured me that providing this service ain't cheap.

She says most of the clients who come to see her are men who are in charge all the time in their lives. "They are the ones who do all the decision making, in their profession, in their home, in their family," she explains. "They come here because they want to let go, to give up responsibility. Others have masochistic fantasies, and they come from all kinds of professions and ages. They want to be under my control, to be tortured."

And Wahl is happy to accommodate.

Epilogue

Since this column was written, Syliva Wahl was deported back to Germany for working in Canada without a visa. Her case was dropped.

A similar case recently went to court in Ontario. It involved Terri-Jean Bedford, who also worked as a professional dominatrix and who was known to her clients as Madame de Sade.

In 1992, police raided her home in a suburb north of Toronto and seized $100,000 worth of dungeon and fantasy-role equipment. She too was charged with operating a common bawdy house. She too argued that what she did did not involve sex, and therefore did not constitute prostitution. The judge begged to differ. After a long and very public trial that spent much time debating exactly where S&M fits into the sexual spectrum and whether or not a dominatrix was basically a whore in leather boots. Bedford was fined $3,000 but was free to go.

Bedford immediately vowed to continue offering her services. Hey, who's going to argue with a woman who tortures people for a living?

Piercing Insights
Turning Your Body into a Metal Deposit

JAY IS HOLDING UP a poster that displays all the genital piercings he offers. He points to one that shows three tiny barbells at three different angles right through the head of a penis. "I've got this one," Jay announces proudly, a wide grin breaking across his classic biker face.

His partner Doreen pipes up from nearby. "I can't stand the guy, but I'll never leave him because of this."

I think they've got an ad campaign there. I was at a tattoo and piercing show at a downtown hotel. Jay and Doreen were there from Wilkes-Barre, Pennsylvania, where their shop Flaming Star Tattoos, carries the current slogan, "Your body is a temple. I'm just here to paint the walls." (I've got the bumper sticker.)

Jay refers to his unique choice of jewelry as his built-in French tickler. "When I'm inside a woman, the tiny steel balls on the end of the posts jiggle around when I move my penis." My, my!

Jay's barbells are actually called ampallangs and, apparently, in the old days, getting one was a standard puberty ritual in more easterly parts of the world. Women could even deny intercourse to guys who didn't have it done. Whaddya think, girls?

While body piercing is all the rage (Jay does about 120-140 body piercings a week), when it comes to puncturing holes in their private parts, Jay says most guys stick to the Prince Albert first time out. That's the ring that goes lengthwise through the urethra at the end of the penis and legend goes that Prince Albert got one to make his royal member behave in those tight little pants. Women's genital piercings don't get any fancy names (though Doreen has dubbed the clitoral piercing Queen Elizabeth. "Fair's fair," she says), but Jay says pierced nipples, navels and clitoral hoods are popular among the ladies.

Apparently one girl who had her hood pierced by him was walking through the mall later and suddenly fell to her knees. Her friends thought she was having a heart attack but when they approached to help, she shooed them away. Turns out, courtesy of her new adornment, she was mid-orgasm, and did not want to be disturbed.

But, unlike we're led to believe, this new-found fun isn't reserved for trend-seeking kids or your run-of-the-mill freaks. As in the days of Prince Albert, when body piercing was reserved for royalty and the rich, the upper echelons are getting in on the action.

Jay does regular private parties (so you can shop in the comfort of your own home) for his wealthy lawyer and doctor friends and, when a local attorney came in to have her lower abdomen pierced, Jay discovered fourteen gold rings on each lip and one through her clitoris. I guess you gotta find ways to amuse yourself during those long days in court.

Kathy is proof of this trend's movement from the margins to the mainstream. She's what you would call your "regular" person and works at a stodgy law firm. None of her colleagues have any idea her nipples, navel, inner and outer labia, and clitoris are packing steel. She got her tongue pierced far enough back so nobody can tell. Nobody, that is, except one of the lawyers in the firm, whom she ran into at a body-piercing social. According to Kathy, he's hauling so much steel, he sets off metal detectors in airports. "But to look at him you'd never know," she adds. "He's very much the pinstripe lawyer."

Kathy too is enthusiastic about the sexual benefits, but says a lot of men are not all that receptive to it. The cringing and expressions of disgust got to be too much, so now she looks for similarly decorated boyfriends. "It's no longer 'What's your sign?' it's, "Do you know what a Prince Albert is?' If they say, 'Wasn't he Queen Victoria's son?' I say, 'Thank you very much, it was nice to meet you' and move on."

But a pierced partner presents its own problems. Yes, Kathy admits, with all that metal clanking around, things get caught sometimes. A bit like two people with braces kissing, I suppose. "It doesn't hurt, though," she insists. "You feel the tug, and you just stop and unhook."

Speaking of getting hooked, Kathy immediately nodded when I asked if she planned on getting more piercings. She's becoming what is known in tattoo and piercing circles as a collector. It's kind of based on the same theory as eating potato chips... you can never stop at just one. "As long as you have space, and you're comfortable, you can collect," Kathy tells me. Hey, some people collect stamps....

"As long as we've been standing, we've been carving out sticks and sticking them into our skin and making marks," says Rob Koss, a tattoo artist at a Chicago shop called Guilty & Innocent, on the current revival of tattooing and piercing. "It seems as though it's core to humankind, the need to ornament our body, whether it's breast enlargements or tattoos or pierced ears."

Beyond the aesthetic value and the supposed enhanced sexual pleasure, Rob admits some people obviously do it for attention or out of human nature to outdo the next guy. "There's also the discipline aspect of it," he adds. "The feeling of overcoming the fear of pain."

As for genital piercing, Rob sees a connection to the popularization of fetish and S&M culture. "It's come out of the dungeon and made its way into fashion and pop culture, and because people who do extreme things have to justify it, they say it feels great, that it makes sex better."

His partner Guy, in the middle of tattooing a guy's arm, offers some piercing insight. "I wore a Prince Albert for a while and I didn't find it improved sex. You also have to pee sitting down so you don't make a mess and you can forget about writing your name in the snow."

Something to think about before you go poking around down there.

Ties That Bind
Bondage 101

"ONE TIME MY PENIS got caught in the zipper of the body bag when this guy was zipping it up," says Max Cita—escape artist, scuba diver, bondage enthusiast and government employee—to a small group of us gathered for one of his regular bondage seminars. "When the guy (referred to as the 'bondage top') zipping it up saw the skin of my penis come through the zipper, I could sense he was gonna pass out." Since Max was strapped into the body bag with his arms restrained inside, he knew he had to talk the guy down and then get him to free willy. "At that point he was more anxious than I was, so I knew I had to take control of the situation even though I was the one in bondage."

Yeah, I think I'd be a little hesitant to rip that zipper down.

The point of Max's story was to illustrate something that gets overlooked in bondage play. Even though the person tying you up is the one in control, they can lose it— more than a mild concern since you'll eventually want them to let you out.

Now I'm not quite ready for body bags, but I'll admit—as I'm sure many will—that at least the idea of a little restraint is exciting. And while fooling around with a few scarves and the bedposts seems harmless, there are still things you need to be concerned about, says Max.

"The first thing most people will do is tie someone spread-eagled on the bed," he says. "But if you stretch someone's arms out too tight and don't give them any elbow room, after thirty minutes they won't be able to breathe." Jesus died from asphyxiation, not from hanging there, Max claims.

Another thing is to learn how to tie knots so they don't dig in, he explained, demonstrating his boy-scout best. "The trick is to tie them so they lie between the joints. You don't want to end up with scars." A nice smooth nylon or cotton rope is best to start with, he adds.

But many novices tend to immediately think of handcuffs when they want to introduce restraint into their sexual play. "Handcuffs work better as a fantasy," according to Max, who makes bondage gear and sells it by mail order through his company, Caught-in-the-Act. "They don't actually play well unless you get the really expensive ones that are designed for this." But even then, he warns, don't ever suspend people with handcuffs.

"The goal is to achieve a safe, sane, consensual experience," Max repeats several times throughout the two-hour session.

This means knowing your limits and being aware of and ready for the potential dangers in what you're doing. Establishing a "safe word" is extremely important, especially if you're playing a game where there has been a prior agreement to ignore your cries to be released. The joke in fetish circles is that Jesus really died on the cross because he forgot his safe word.

As much as I know you'd like to run out right now and buy yourself a $1,200 body bag and zip yourself up for a day or two, you gotta start slow and work your way up, cautions Max. "People who are into bondage see these neat pictures in magazines of heavy, heavy bondage—people hanging upside down and stuff—and think, 'Neat, I'd like to do that,' but these are people with 15 years' experience."

Max is quite a fan of male genital bondage. "Tying your genitals gives you a wicked erection," he smiles. "It's a bit more limited for women." (Yeah, it's a bugger trying to get that little knot tied around your clitoris without it slippin' off.)

Again, though, as appealing as it sounds, no marathons. "Twenty minutes, max," he says. By way of demonstration, the video in the background shows a guy decked out head-to-toe in latex with only his weenie hanging out. The penis is bound with rope and tied off from a ring piercing the head to a belt around his knees. Meanwhile, his partner is using two vibrators on the bound penis, and tapping nipples and other body parts through the latex. I dunno. I guess that could be fun.

Max introduces his partner, Suni MX, into the seminar by demonstrating their 100-foot rope trick. The rope is strategically knotted so that when she's bound the knots nestle neatly into her vagina and butthole.

Suni wasn't into bondage before she met Max. She took a lot of flack from people when she met him three years ago. "They wondered how I could go out with someone like that, but he was more caring than any lover I had ever been with." He even gave her a studded collar for Valentine's Day.

And they didn't do it on the first date. "You have to build trust, and respect limits," she says. "He was very kind."

Since restriction of movement and sensory deprivation are the big turn-ons in most bondage, you better trust the person you're doing it with. You don't want to be hooded and gagged and suddenly hear them rummaging through the knife drawer in the kitchen.

One other rule Max insists upon: "First drink of the day ends the play." Same goes for drugs. While sensory deprivation is the goal, you need your senses about you first in order to deprive them. Oh yeah, and if you're tying someone up, let them go pee first. In case of emergency, Caught-in-the-Act does sell catheters.

Aside from the penis cages, mail bags, straightjackets, hand, head and foot stocks he's built, Max has enough architectural know-how to design fully-equipped bondage jungle gyms that can disappear into closets, or a bondage-friendly suburban living room that can be neighbour-friendly in an instant. When I met them, he and Suni were in the process of building themselves a custom-designed bondage bungalow. At the time, they were stuck in a two-room apartment with little space for all their toys. But you should have seen their bed!

Undie World

Your Latest Fantasy, Now Available on Video

"NO GOLDEN SHOWERS or toilet stuff." That's where James, the man behind Premier Productions—a made-to-pleasure custom-video company—draws the line. The catalogue advertises "lace & lingerie videos and photo-sets for the true connoisseur." Nothing illegal either—no kids or animals—and no hardcore stuff. There are no men in his videos (except one that features a guy cross-dressing for his girlfriend), and James won't tape (I swear there is a tinge of embarrassment in his voice)—"you know, uh, oral sex"—between women.

The forty-something former airline pilot doesn't sound like someone who spends his days videotaping women in their under-wear and distributing videos with titles like *Panties, Panties, Panties* and *Curlers in My Pussy Hair*. Over the phone, the guy sounds downright, well, homey. A bit like Mr Rogers, only not as sleazy.

Premier began as a nice family business. James started it in 1989 when his brother—who had been running a similar biz for 15 years in California—couldn't handle all of his Canadian orders. When the airline downsized James into early retirement, this side business took off. Premier's catalogue features 65 video titles and

35 still photo-sets. "It's not as big as triple X—that is, hardcore stuff—which is still what 80-90 percent of guys want, but there's a niche for lace and lingerie."

"Tan" pantyhose is popular I notice, flipping through the catalogue. "Yeah, and taupe," he laughs. But slips are the real big seller, James tells me.

"I do slip videos for a customer in Detroit constantly. He sends the slips—which are like size 48, so you know the guy probably wears them himself—and I tape women trying them on and rubbing them over their bodies. I send the slips back with the tape. He pays $300 bucks for a 30-minute video."

But Premier's undie-niche started getting crowded, and James decided to expand. Premier now offers a whole range of fetish videos from the standards (feet, voyeurism, nurses, maids, nuns) to more unusual requests. Smoking videos for example. Yes, as in, videos of women smoking.

"A guy in New York does a newsletter called *Smoke Signals* specifically geared to people with a smoking fetish," James, a non-smoker, explains. "When he requested a video from me, I was hesitant at first because I didn't think there was a market for it. But since he was paying for it, I did it. Now I'm amazed at how these things sell."

James gets about four or five orders a week for his smoking videos, which are advertised through the newsletter. "I get orders from Italy and all over the world," he says, sounding as surprised as I am. I know smoking in public is becoming taboo these days, but really… you gotta wonder… why?

"I don't know," James laughs (he laughs a lot). "I don't question anything—to each to his own, I say. Maybe it's a 'bad girls smoke' thing, I couldn't even begin to understand why."

And it's not like they want the girls to do anything unusual with their cig. They just wanna see her smoke, real hard.

"They're not interested in nudity," he explains. "The first smoking video I shot of a girl playing with herself while she smoked was my worst seller. My best seller is of a girl dressed in lingerie with her top on, smoking."

Apparently, she gives good inhale. Customers also appreciate her intense exhaling and French inhales. Another guy ordered a tape of a woman smoking and wanted her to hack all the way through. "That one's popular, too."

James relies solely on customer suggestions for scenarios. "Since I'm not into this stuff, I find it very difficult to come up with new material using my own brain." Once he fills a customer's special request, the title is made available through his catalogue for about $30 each. But the price of the original product varies, depending on props, content or the going rate on horse manure.

Yup, one guy paid $1200 for a video of a woman walking through horse shit with her boots on and then ordering him to lick it off. What was that line again? Oh yeah: To each his own, to each his own….

"The guy saved for about a year to have that video done," James tells me. "He couldn't buy it anywhere."

While I'm happy you could cater to this fellow's needs, James, don't you ever feel a little strange about what you do?

"I have no moral qualms about it," he says. Though he admits his wife's a little put off by her hubby's career change.

"Her attitude is 'Do what you have to do but don't tell me about it,'" James tells me. "And she enjoys the nice vehicles and flying first class wherever she goes. But she thinks what I do is degrading to women. I tell her women get used for advertising all the time. And they don't put a big, fat, hairy girl in the convertible —they use a model."

And you, sir, do you think it's degrading to women?

"To tell you the truth, no. My wife and I are in our forties and I think we're from a different era," he says. "A lot of these women are in their twenties and they just think differently. Nudity does not bother them at all."

And Walker insists the women in his videos (he gets them from modeling agencies) know the job involves nudity and have final say over what they will and won't do.

"Some girls won't go further than straight nudity," he says. "Some won't masturbate on camera—even though it is faked for the videos—and that's fine."

As for his clients… "I think many of these guys' home lives leave a little to be desired," James speculates. "I think a lot of them are lonely souls or have wives who aren't interested in catering to their special requests.

"And if a guy discovers, 'Gee I'm not the only one who likes to watch girls smoke, maybe I'm not so weird,' that might be a positive thing."

It's certainly positive for business.

I wonder what James thinks about the video-game theory. You know, you master one level, get bored, and have to move on to the next. "Yeah, I wonder about that just like you," James admits: "Things get boring so you have to crank up the weird level a notch or two. I really don't know. I haven't tried to analyze it. I do what I do and distribute that catalogue and don't put a lot of deep thought into it."

Ironically, he might be his own best example of the video-game theory. "I used to be surprised by how weird some of the requests were, now I'm just like, 'Whup, that's a weird one.'"

Like the guy who wanted a video of a woman in a full leg cast walking around on crutches. He didn't do it. Not because it was too weird, but cast material is tricky stuff and he was worried about injuring the model if it hardened too quickly. "The guy offered to come and help, but I was like, 'No thanks.'"

To each his own, to each....

Gender Neutral
Sometimes, Boys Will Be Girls

To DERMABLEND or not to Dermablend, that is the question—at least in cross-dressing circles. Roxy's just got a light covering today. The heavy pancake makeup doesn't exactly achieve a peaches-and-cream complexion, but what's a girl to do when you've got five o'clock shadow pushing through. "I didn't have time to give myself a close shave before you arrived," Roxy tells me. After all, dressed down in a sweatshirt, sneakers, and a smart red denim mini, Roxy had planned to spend the day unglamorously pulling up weeds in the back yard. He's the handyman about the house.

He's also the girl behind the counter in Take a Walk on the Wild Side, a Toronto boutique catering to cross-dressers and drag queens, owned by Roxy's wife, Paddy Aldridge.

They were married on Halloween. Growing up, Halloween was pretty important to Roxy. Under the false eyelashes and flowing blond wig, Roxy is actually Tom, a straight guy who loves women so-o-o much he likes to dress like them. As a budding cross-dresser in small-town Ontario, fright night was the one time a year he could dress to the nines as a woman and be accepted. Naturally, they were both brides for the wedding.

Tom, forty-nine, had pretty much given up on having a relationship when he met Paddy at the store several years ago. He already had one marriage fail because his wife couldn't deal with his desire to dress up as a woman. "Then I met Paddy, who is bisexual and was married to a post-operative transsexual, that is, a man who had changed sex to a woman."

Yeah, I was a little confused at this point too. And I had the added bonus of having this told to me by a distinctly male voice coming out of a perfectly painted mouth.

When you think about it, Paddy and Roxy are the perfect match. "I'm man and woman enough for Paddy."

Paddy agrees. "I'm attracted to Tom, who fixes things around the house, and I'm attracted to Roxy, who is kind and submissive and does what I say," she laughs.

But more important, Paddy made it okay for Roxy, Tom's feminine persona, to shine. "Roxy has taken over," he says. "I paint my toenails, and I shave my body completely. I also sleep in a nightie, just as I did when I was a child."

In fact, there are many signs from Tom's childhood that explain his desire to live as Roxy. His father was never around and he was raised by his mother, her three sisters, and a grandmother who were very much into fashion, Hollywood, and all that "girlie stuff." "I learned to sew before I rode a bike," Roxy, uh, Tom tells me. "I never did team sports or guy things and I always wanted to be Darlene of the Mousketeers."

His parents didn't discourage his behaviour. "One day, when

I was dressing up for Halloween, I heard my father tell my mother, 'Marg, I think we've got the daughter we've always wanted.'"

It wasn't until he wore nail polish to kindergarten one day that he realized there was anything different about this.

But while both straight and gay people often presume that a man in women's clothing is automatically gay, Tom says he has never considered having sex with men. In fact, he says, 99 percent of the shop's clientele are heterosexual males.

"And I'm not a female trapped in a man's body," he adds. "I simply prefer the female gender. I don't do it to entice men to hit on me and I try not to offend women or gay men by dressing this way. I do it to express myself and to be more intimate with my partner."

Roxy refers to Virginia Prince, a pioneer in cross-dressing circles from France who is in his eighties. Prince abandoned his masculine identity entirely twenty-seven years ago. "Virginia believes gender is learned like a language," says Roxy. "While your sex is between your legs, your gender is between your ears. He abandoned his masculine gender because he found it too stressful to live up to."

Roxy, too, believes men are more restricted in their gender roles. Not only do women have more options in what they can wear, but a man displaying stereotypically feminine traits such as crying or being more gentle is less acceptable than is a women displaying traditionally masculine traits like aggressiveness.

And what's even scarier for a straight man than being perceived as feminine is being perceived as gay, he adds. "Ironically, when I'm Roxy, being with Paddy makes me a lesbian," he ponders. "But all these labels are bullshit."

So how does he think he cuts it as a woman? "I'm 6'1" (and that's before the size 12 D heels) and weigh 225 pounds. I mean, I'm a cross-dressed man," he admits. "I have no intentions of passing as a woman."

It all sounds pretty logical, but I have one small beef. Femininity is about a lot more than throwing on some makeup, heels, and a wig. In fact, I can't help but feel that most cross-dressers end up coming across as parodies of a woman; overstated, and not like many women I know.

When I express my concern to Roxy, he counters that simply wearing the clothes changes how you act as well as your attitude. "If you wear high heels for nine hours, the walk and the gestures develop," he says. I still wasn't sure I bought it. Then a friend suggested that perhaps it was a bit like lighting candles and dimming the lights to create romance. It isn't romance itself, but it shifts your thinking in that direction. I suppose I can buy that.

Man Trouble

Teenie Weenie

Let Dr. Stubbs Enhance Your Manhood

Yes, okay, I admit it. There is that moment—the first time you get naked with a guy and see his penis—a moment of pleasant surprise, or that slight sinking feeling when you know you'll be giving your girlfriends the universal pinkie symbol the next day.

Size does matter. There. I said it. But does it matter enough for a guy to shell out almost $4,300 dollars and risk, at worst, death, or (perhaps even worse) ending up with an elephant-man penis, all for a bigger one? At the very least, there's a lot of discomfort involved. Surely it'd be safer and more economical to get creative. It's not the meat, it's the motion and all that, you know?

"If a penile augmentation cost $100,000, I'd still do it," said one gentleman, who was augmented from four and three-quarters to six and a half inches by a cosmetic surgeon in Toronto named, I kid you not, Dr. Stubbs. "You only live once. There's no second chance," says our first lucky contestant.

He says he started feeling insecure about the size of his penis about ten years ago, and was thrilled to discover that Dr. Stubbs could do something about it. After two operations—one to lengthen and one to widen—and several weeks of recovery, he was ready to test drive his new toy.

"I'm very happy with the results. I feel more confident. Women like it bigger and wider."

We'd also like it if potato chips were considered health food. Truth be told, admits Dr. Stubbs, none of the guys who come for the procedure are there as a result of complaints from their female partners. (What can I say, we're raised to be polite.)

"Most guys who want the surgery have average penises but got insecure about them somewhere along the way," he says. "We call it the locker-room syndrome."

Since the fall of 1993, when Dr. Stubbs returned from China where he learned his technique from—get this—Dr. Long, Dr. Stubbs has performed hundreds of penile augmentations at his private clinic, the Cosmetic Surgicentre in Toronto's wealthy Yorkville neighbourhood.

Unlike most cosmetic surgeons in North America, who simply inject liquid-fat cells from other parts of the body into the penis to pump it up, Dr. Stubbs cuts loose the part of the penis inside the pelvis and lets it enjoy the outside world. A few nips and tucks and you're on your way. If you want more girth, he'll either inject liquid-fat cells or do something called a dermal-fat grafting, whereby the fat cells are still attached to a layer of skin and transplanted into the penis to make it thicker. "The problem with the popular American technique of simply injecting the penis with fat cells is that they are unpredictable," says Dr. Stubbs, taking a break from a busy day of breast implants, nose jobs and facelifts.

"Injected fat cells can die or move around and be reabsorbed into the body, eventually returning the penis to its former size or in some cases leaving it deformed."

Results vary, but Stubbs says he can add anywhere from a half to two inches in length. "You can't turn a four-inch penis into a 10-inch penis," he explains. "Our maximum result has been two-and-a-half inches, but I consider a one-inch gain a success." And apparently, the bigger the penis is to start, the smaller the gain.

He has no "you have to be this small to ride this ride" requirement, but Stubbs spends a lot of time with patients before he agrees to do the surgery to make sure they're psychologically and physically up for it. So while Stubbs is now doing two to three penile enlargements a week, he says he turns down about 75 percent of the men who come to him.

"Initially, it was novel, and guys who were already big wanted to see if they could be bigger, maybe because they didn't want someone else to get ahead of them in line," says Stubbs. "In some cases, young guys come in because they figure the reason their girlfriends don't have an orgasm is because of the size of their penis. They just need to be told the facts of life."

Dr. Stubbs also turns away overweight patients and smokers as high-risk candidates for the procedure.

After the surgery, weights are hung from the penis to stretch the scar and the penis, and to prevent it from retreating to its former home behind the pelvic bone. The weights are what cause much of the actual growth, which freaks some guys out because they think it won't stop, says Stubbs. Of course, some are very pleased by this, he adds, figuring it'll be hanging out the bottom of their trousers in a few weeks. And no intense workouts or sex for at least a month.

Needless to say, the whole thing can be a little traumatic. Beyond the natural swelling and bruising after the operation, complications can range from bleeding, skin loss, loss of sensation, and a feeling like you just hauled a 747 with your dick.

Enter Elizabeth Flanagan, the Florence Nightingale of penile augmentations. A registered nurse with a Master's degree in science and nursing, she runs a cozy little B&B called Butternut House in Toronto that puts plenty of Dr. Stubbs' patients up after surgery. She points out that it is not a licensed recovery facility; she is simply a friendly innkeeper (ordinary guests assume these men are, well, ordinary guests) who is skilled to deal with any complications these guys might have after surgery. For $850 for three nights, patients get coddled and tended to hand and penis. "It makes them feel like little boys with mom bringing them chicken soup to make them feel better."

Flanagan says patients from nineteen to seventy-two years of age come from around the world and from all walks of life; from famous people (she wouldn't reveal any names) to businessmen to working-class stiffs.

Oh yeah, all-night erections are another potential post-op problem that, uh, comes up. "This can be pretty scary for them, but I have analgesics on hand to deal with it," says Flanagan. "And

I'm in 24-hour contact with Dr. Stubbs if there are any serious complications." And she has cable and colour TV!

Flanagan agrees that in many cases men put themselves through this, not because a girlfriend has complained or that they were so small to begin with, but because they've experienced some psychological trauma that has made them insecure about the size of their penis.

"Maybe someone pointed it out and ridiculed them about it," she says. When I suggested that perhaps they might want to get over it rather than go through all this, she says, quite simply, "Most of these guys think 'Yeah, I could go through years of therapy but it's not going to lengthen my penis.' It's as simple as that."

A Tough Pill to Swallow
Helping Guys Who Can't Get it Up

RICHARD CASEY makes his living giving men hard-ons.

"I can give an erection to a dead man," boasts the founder of the Male Health Centres, which run three clinics in Ontario specializing in men's sexual health problems. Prostate disease and erectile dysfunction (you're not allowed to call it impotence anymore—too negative, makes guys feel like losers) are the main focus of the clinics.

According to Joan Graham, the general manager of the Centres, an estimated 20-30 million men, or about one in eight, in North America can't get it up. And it's not just old guys, as most people think. While 25 percent of men lose it by age seventy-five, at least eight percent of young adult men aren't as virile as they once were.

That's because the penis is apparently one of the first things to go if life is giving you a hard time (I promise I will try to resist the inevitable penis jokes that are sure to, oh no... arise), says Graham. "I'm surprised by the number of men I see with histories of good sexual performance who lose it with just one or two setbacks."

Divorce and job loss are biggies. (I'm biting my tongue...)

"One guy didn't even lose his job," Graham continues. "They were restructuring the company, and he was worried that he might lose his job and became impotent just because of the anxiety."

Same with divorce, she says, "For a guy in his forties, it's a real attack on the way he sees himself." And, in many cases, it's also a big surprise. "Often, she's been sending signals for a long time, he hasn't been paying attention, and then, suddenly, she says, 'I'm leaving.' This can be devastating, and often he finds he can't get an erection with a new partner because he hasn't resolved the relationship with his ex-wife."

In the case of older men, sometimes you're just not the anytime/anywhere guy you used to be. "As men enter their forties and fifties, they need to be in the mood as well," says Casey, a urologist who got into the male sexual dysfunction field in the early 1980s when he realized very few doctors wanted to deal with these problems. "When you're young, it's the first item on your 'things to do today' list: Have sex, eat..."

The problem isn't always psychological. Diabetes, heart attacks, spinal injury, basically anything that slows down blood flow can leave you limp. And, since penis arteries are relatively small, anything that affects your arteries will have its way with your wee-wee. Smoking, drinking and greasy food will all threaten your masculinity, boys.

Casey says psychological and physical causes are split about 50/50 but often it's a combination of the two.

"A guy can have mild erectile problems as a result of smoking or blood pressure pills, and then they have one or two failures and pretty soon they become a self-fulfilling prophesy." In other words they become so worried about getting it up that they can't get it up.

"One guy was feeling okay until one day his wife said, 'I don't think you're as hard as you used to be,'" Casey recounts. "He's been useless since. It can happen as easily as that." (Touchy, touchy, boys.)

Casey says with the choice of treatments available today, erectile problems can be cured in about 95 percent of cases, but some men are too embarrassed to ask for help. Often, if they do ask their family doctor for help, they are simply told they need to relax, or if they're older, "he's told he should just be thankful to be alive, or that he shouldn't worry about sex at 60."

No wonder men were falling over themselves to get a hold of Viagra, the little blue magic impotency pill, when it was approved for the U.S. market earlier this year (Actually, calling it an impotency pill is misleading. This thing is potent.)

Who can blame them? If I couldn't get it up for years (who cares if the reason is psychological or physical) and suddenly taking a pill could solve my problem, I'd be right in there. It sure beats the options. I wouldn't want to be sticking a needle in my dick, either (a penile injection, along with vacuum pumps and erectile surgical implants were the leading treatments before Viagra came along).

I admit too, as a woman, if my date couldn't get it up on a regular basis, I'd be thrilled to discover Viagra. I love cunnilingus and all the rest of it as much as the next gal, but sometimes you just really want to bonk. And it really does feel better when he's fully at attention. I also sleep better on a nice, hard bed than a soft mattress. An added bonus with Viagra is that it takes stimulation and about an hour to kick in. Foreplay anyone?

So a few guys with heart conditions croaked from all the excitement. They shoulda read the warnings. Nitrates and Viagra don't mix. Not surprisingly, women are test driving Viagra and, aside from the blinding headaches and blue vision, most of the women in the cases I've read about thought it was great. At least when it didn't make them too nauseous to screw. Apparently, though, while Viagra definitely makes a girl more tingly, it doesn't guarantee her orgasm. Figures, eh? We women have been complaining about our difficulty achieving orgasm for years and they come up with a pill that helps guys out. Because, you know, they just don't get to have enough orgasms.

As for guys, they can't get enough of the stuff, even if they don't necessarily need it. Viagra sold more in its first six months than any other drug that's ever been released—up to 40,000 prescriptions a day—one source said. The fact that it hasn't yet been approved here in Canada hasn't stopped us from getting our hands on it. (Just another item to pick up on cross-border shopping sprees.) Oddly enough in France, where it has just recently been

Casey has been criticized for running "an erection mill" because approved, sales don't seem to be as brisk as in the U.S.

Blame it on the North American high-fat diet. Or maybe French men really are better lovers. American men seem to still think good sex is about how good his erection is. They're educated in the school of harder, faster and all-night-long? Or is it that having a super-hard dick makes them feel like more of a man?

The dictionary describes impotence as weakness, ineffectiveness and powerlessness. And they're not necessarily referring to a man's penis. Maybe Viagra is the answer to a growing sense of powerlessness that men are feeling, the fact that women are controlling the agenda in so many ways these days—especially when it comes to sex. We're telling men what we want, and how we want it. I guess it's tough not to feel a little inadequate. And why deal with it when a little blue pill can make you feel in control again? Not all of us have a 21-year-old intern available to reaffirm our virility.

But maybe that's too harsh. After all, when it comes to sex, we're probably all feeling a little impotent. It's hard not to when there's an entire industry out there to help us improve our obviously less-than-adequate sex lives.

Hell, why not come up with a pill that simulates sex entirely? Take the performance pressure off everyone. Imagine all the time and effort it would save. Sex would always be mind-blowing, no one would feel inadequate, and we could all catch up on our sleep.

Marathon Men
Do We Really Want You to Last All Night Long?

ATELOPUS FROGS have intercourse for as long as six months. That's gotta chafe after a while. Granted, they don't spend the entire time actually boinking. According to Adrian Forsyth, in his book. *A Natural History of Sex*, it's more of an overly enthusiastic measure taken on the part of Mr. Frog to guarantee that his sperm will be first in line to inseminate Ms. Frog's eggs as soon as she lays them.

Apparently, he latches on, then just wastes away and dies, leaving only a seminal contribution to the future of his fellow amphibs behind. Admittedly, there are probably some folks out there who might be mildly intrigued by the idea of giving up their life for six straight months of sex, but I personally find it a bit extreme. Especially since you don't even get to live to see your little tadpole's first little-league game. Scientists aren't completely sure why certain species feel the male has to be offed in order to procreate, though theory has it that hanging out and letting your mate eat you is considered a small investment if it gives you a better shot at every egg she releases.

These frogs aren't the only marathon-sex maniacs. Certain flies (appropriately known as "love bugs" in areas of the U.S.) have massive bug orgies and screw for up to 56 hours at a time. Not a bad life, considering they only survive two to five days as adults.

These are exceptions, however. Most animals are much more into quickies. I watched a young ram, uh, ramming my brother's ewe last winter. The ewe seemed utterly freaked while that eager young stud chased her around the pen trying to stick his thing in her like a fifteen-year-old guy on his first time out. The poor thing didn't look like she was enjoying it much. I wanted to take Rambo aside and discuss some foreplay technique.

Chimpanzees—our closest relatives— are also in and out of there in a flash. Wild animals have to be quick. In the jungle, taking your time with sex might get you killed.

Maybe it's got something to do with trying to distance ourselves as much as possible from our furry friends, or maybe, at some point, someone thought intercourse stood a chance as an official Olympic sport for men, but somewhere along the line male endurance became a major goal in human sexual intercourse.

However it happened, we've now become obsessed with training men to last all night long. Books and manuals abound with tips on how to keep going till she's raw and chafed: the squeeze technique, the stop-start technique; wear double condoms, numb it with cream, try different positions, develop your PC muscles, think about your grandmother while you're having sex.

I'm not saying you should be aping our cousins, but sometimes, well, I just want you to come already!

In 1938, studies by Alfred Charles Kinsey showed that 75

percent of men ejaculate within two to three minutes of vaginal penetration. Apparently, men slowed down a little by the 1960s, when Masters and Johnson put the average time at two-and-a-half to three-and-a-half minutes.

Compare this to that "definitive survey" that came out of the University of Chicago few years ago. Of the men polled, 69 percent thought they spent 15 minutes to an hour on penetration, while 20 percent said it lasted longer than an hour.

An hour!? Trust me, there are times when going that extra mile is desirable (usually signified by the bite marks in your arm when you suddenly stop or slow down, or by the words "Don't stop!" being screamed in your ear), but pumping away for an hour? Can you say "yeast infection"?

Personally, I don't know how guys do it. A minute and a half on top and I'm pooped—if my knees haven't buckled already. But I've been with guys who pump away, sweating like pigs until their knees are raw. The expression on their faces is definitely not conveying pleasure—it looks more like they're bench pressing 200 pounds. That's when I usually put him in a leg hold and gently whisper "sloooow dowwwn." I mean, if he's not enjoying it, I have to presume he's doing it because he thinks that's what he's supposed to do—or worse yet—that's what we want. Well, he's not and I don't.

A big part of the problem is that sex is still defined as intercourse—the amount of time it was in her.

What ever happened to quality, not quantity? And there is

absolutely no rule that says once it's in, it has to stay there. And I'd take three minutes of the old in-out stretched out over a period of one hour, with a bunch of other stuff in between, over 30 minutes of straight humping any day.

Male PMS?
It Might Be That Time of the Month for Him Too

GIRLS, what would you think if someone told you that it was merely coincidence that you suddenly burst into tears while watching "Friends" and then just happened to get your period the next day?

If you were a woman in the company of other women you'd no doubt recognize the correlation. If you were a woman talking to a guy, of course, you'd insist it had nothing to do with your period and get angry at him for automatically thinking that. If you were a guy who's been through that latter scenario, you'd say, "What's wrong, baby?" while thinking, "She must be getting her period."

That's because we've been led to believe for so long that our mood cycles and our menstrual cycles go hand-in-hand, says Tannis MacBeth Williams, who's been studying menstrual cycles since the mid-80s. Well guess what guys? According to her latest research, you're just as likely to get PMS—Premenstrual Syndrome, for those of you not from around here—as we are. If you had a period, that is. Which some men did, well, a fake one anyway, in a study Williams did with three of her colleagues at the University of British Columbia. They were in town presenting their research at, and I kid you not, the Biannual Conference for the Society of Menstrual Cycle Research.

Let me try and explain. Williams & Co took a bunch of women and men and got them to chart their physical and mental states every day for about four months. They had to keep track of things like their moods, their quality of sleep, if they felt good about what they ate that day, how turned-on they were, their ability to concentrate and their relationships with partners and co-workers.

Just to keep things fair, the men were also assigned an arbitrary 28-day menstrual cycle (without the muss and fuss of an actual period, of course). The researchers also kept track of the lunar cycles, you know, full-moon, half-moon, etc. This is one thing that has been tossed around, especially in feel-good, New-Age circles, as something that men and women may share when it comes to feeling the weirdies for apparently no reason at all throughout the month.

What they found, according to Williams, is that both the men and women in the study had cycles, but they appeared to be completely individual and had nothing to do with the moon, the stars, our hormones, when we bleed or what's on TV.

For example, just as many men experienced "premenstrual lows," that is, they felt down in the few days before their fake period, as women who felt low before their real period. In other words, they had what we call PMS.

"The stereotype is that men don't fluctuate and that's healthy, and the stereotype is that women all fluctuate in the same way, related to their menstrual cycle, and that's unhealthy," says Williams.

In fact, while 70 percent of the men and women had mood cycles, these cycles didn't consistently follow the pattern of any of our cultural beliefs, be it PMS, weekend highs, Monday blues or buggy full-moon stuff. For some guys, Thursdays rocked.

So does this mean we should toss the whole PMS concept out the window? It does seem maybe we've been going down the wrong path in trying to find a biological explanation for what we've come to call PMS, says Williams. "Women are experiencing cycles across their menstrual cycle, but they aren't having stereotypical cycles; some of them are having premenstrual terrifics, some of them having a mid-cycle miserable. It's different for every woman."

This means all those hormone charts they've been showing us to try and explain why we feel the way we do are crap. "Nobody's come up with any evidence linking hormones to women's experiences. There's no treatment or even consensus. And none of it explains why men would have mood cycles," answers Williams.

Williams' theory is that these cycles are naturally occurring, but not necessarily biological. "Human beings have a natural ebb and flow in their body," she says. "People feel different at different seasons; sometimes we want to eat more, sometimes we have more energy, so that's all that I think that it is. It probably has more to do with what's going on in our lives than hormones.

"We have to rethink what's healthy and normal," Williams continues. "To have PMS clinics that treat large numbers of women as if this is abnormal and unhealthy, with the goal of trying to eliminate fluctuation, seems unwise."

I can just hear all you bloated, cranky women out there, screaming, "Bullshit!" But Williams insists that, for women who experience a lot of physical changes during their menstrual cycle, they begin to connect them with certain moods. We're not allowed to just be moody, so if we blame it on our periods, we have a legitimate reason for feeling out of sorts. On the other hand, it also gets used against us, the aforementioned "she must be getting her period," every time you're in a bad mood.

Williams said the men in the study were pretty stunned when they were told they also had these cycles. "Of course, it wasn't how they'd been taught to think about themselves," she points out. "The women weren't surprised because the culture has been telling women this all along. They were surprised, however, to find out that their cycles weren't stereotypically connected to their menstrual cycle."

What was also interesting, says Williams, was that quite a few of the men said they were relieved, because they'd had the gut feeling that they do have cycles and ups and downs, but they haven't, in a way, been given permission to acknowledge that.

Maybe it would help if guys could get in touch with their cycles too. We'd feel less defective as women because guys would have the same excuse for acting weird once in a while. We could all blame our cycles.

Watching football will never be the same now, will it, boys... Kleenex?

"Nice" Guys
Why Can't Sensitive Guys Get Laid?

"HE'S A REEEALLY nice guy, funny, considerate, a real sweetheart. I don't know what it is, but I'm just not turned on by him."

Sound familiar?

Why go for funny, sweet, considerate when we can go for indifferent, self-centred and manipulative? So much sexier.

Johnny O'Neil wanted to know just what is up with that. He's a Montreal video maker who poked his camera in people's faces trying to get to the bottom of the question that has been weighing heavy on his gentle mind. Why can't nice guys get laid?

O'Neil is a self-proclaimed "sensitive guy" who has a hard time getting any. Well, he spent one too many days in I-like-you-as-a-friend purgatory. He wanted answers.

"Do I have to be an asshole to get women to sleep with me?" he asked me in despair.

Nice guys don't get laid? Over half of the 22 people he asked on camera said it's true, only four said it's false, and five said maybe. With these kinds of results, I figure he deserved an explanation. Especially being such a nice guy and all.

Unfortunately, I'm still trying to come up with one. I could just say women are all liars and, that while we say we want to be with someone who's sensitive, we really are just hooked on being treated like shit. But that would be admitting defeat. Besides, I think it's a little more complicated.

Maybe it's our fault for trying to teach an old dog new tricks. Can't blame a girl for trying. But while our lofty feminist attempts to encourage men to get in touch with their feelings have resulted in a few changed diapers, some badly washed dishes, maybe even a remembered birthday here and there, it's also gotten us into a whole new mess. Some of you have learned the tricks better than others and we've become confused.

As one of O'Neil's "sensitive" subjects revealed, "If you can pretend to be sensitive, the world's your oyster."

Ah, the old asshole disguised as a sensitive guy routine. A wonderful combination of what we're used to and what we're trying to find. This guy learns how to push all the right buttons without ever really having to be genuinely sensitive. He's charming, thoughtful, tells you how beautiful you are, and is probably professing his love to you within 24 hours. You let down your guard, let him know you care, and whammo, you're sucked in. From then on—if you ever hear from the guy again—you'll only get glimmers of that sweet soul, just enough to keep you hanging. Why do we fall for it?

Why love when you can long instead? Misery and anguish can make you feel so alive, while the predictability of steady, supportive love can get tiresome. No tension. Why settle for a middle ground when you can live from one extreme to the other? A life full of sweeties who we wish we could love more to the jerks we wish we could love less.

Oh yes, then there's the sex. Unfortunately, nice guys have earned a reputation for being boring in bed. Maybe it's because nice guys worry so much about well, being nice. "I worry about whether I am being too aggressive or not aggressive enough," O'Neil confesses.

Nice guys don't want to be daring or suggestive, because they're so worried about offending us; meanwhile, we don't want to say anything about how boring the sex is, cause they're too nice.

See, but this is the problem with a lot of nice guys. They're too nice. They're so worried about what we think, their own personalities disappear in the process. Or worse, there's the "super-sensitive" guy. This is the guy who identifies with your struggles, calls himself a "feminist," then wants a pat on the back for it to confirm his sensitivity. In his attempt to be one of the girls, he makes unsolicited comments like, "Men are such pigs." He figures this will make us like him. This is not nice or sensitive, this is selfish. If we wanted to go out with one of the girls, we'd go for the real McCoy. Like the sensitive asshole act, we are keen to the fact that this is merely a ploy to win us over. Except, unlike the sensitive asshole who keeps us hooked by not wanting it (and the great sex), this type turns us off because he wants it too much. It's embarrassing.

Of course, this all makes things kinda rough for the genuinely sensitive guy. All two of you, according to one of O'Neil's male interviewees. You get confused too. We want you to be vulnerable, then accuse you of being weak. Silly us, thinking you could find the balance.

So nice guys sit around and watch jerks get all the action and it smarts. I suppose you could simply learn the tricks too. But consider this, sensitive guys. It's probably easier to be a little less sensitive (take it from us girls, we practice it all our lives) than it is for ice man to warm up a little.

The first just takes practice, the second takes courage.

Girlie Bits

G, Is It Whiz?

The Elusive Search for the Female G-spot

THE FIRST TIME I ejaculated it took me by surprise. I was about sixteen and enjoying a pretty healthy sex life with my first real boyfriend. He thought I had peed. I suspected it was orgasm-related (it sure felt good, and by age sixteen you pretty much know your pee), but his suggestion made me wonder and suddenly feel embarrassed. I shyly told him that it felt more like what I imagined a guy must feel, intense build-up and then gush, the release. I didn't understand how it had happened, but I knew it wasn't pee. He thought that was pretty neat but I still got the feeling he didn't quite believe me.

He's not alone.

Sex researchers and therapists have been debating this one for years. Back in the 1960s, Masters & Johnson, the biggies when it comes to shaping the way the medical world views sexuality, described female ejaculation as "an erroneous but widespread concept." They blamed the release of fluid on "urinary stress incontinence." You know, like dribbling when you cough or sneeze. M&J have changed their tune since then but the so-called experts still won't outright admit the G-spot exists.

Shannon Bell thinks this is crap. She doesn't need scientific proof. She, like me, has chosen to rely on first-hand information. Bell even held a series of female ejaculation workshops (complete with demonstration) to dispel the "myth of the G-spot." A friend of mine attended one and admitted that, while it was a bit bizarre to watch someone jerk off in front of a roomful of men and women, the workshop was incredibly enlightening.

"It tapped into how we're fed information, not just 'how do you find the G-spot?'" she told me, over the phone. Finding it's the easy part, she said. "We're always told how difficult it is to find the G-spot, but it's like you can't see the forest for the trees, it's right there, you can't miss it if you try." She knows this because a woman in the workshop demonstrated how to use a speculum on yourself and then invited everyone to check it out. "So, what did it look like?" "Uh, Jos, I'm at work."

The most I managed to get out of her was that it was like a bump on the upper wall just inside the vagina. To discover your own, you need only put your finger inside and you can feel it. The area feels a bit like the roof of your mouth and the raised area is actually your urethral sponge (it was called the G-Spot after Dr Ernst Grafenberg who "discovered" it in the 50s). This sponge swells with fluid when stimulated. Pressure on this from fingers, toes, penises and other fun things can make you spurt.

Still, although science has come up with some proof that enzymes in this fluid are similar to male ejaculate (without the seed, of course), they still don't want to recognize it as female ejaculation. Because it's a part of the anatomy that remains vaguely defined, unfocused-on, and not taught about, women end up thinking, 'I think I've found it, but I'm not sure.'

"Yeah, it's like, 'no it can't exist, because science says it doesn't' but yet there it is, I've seen it," my friend agrees. "It's as if they don't want to acknowledge that women have the same ability to ejaculate as men."

In an essay called "Feminist Ejaculations," Shannon Bell traces the history of attitudes and theories about female ejaculation and the G-spot. In Greek and Roman times, Bell writes, doctors weren't debating whether female ejaculate existed but rather whether it had procreative properties. The theory went that making babies required both male and female "semen." Aristotle was the first to challenge this, saying the female discharge was not seminal but simply part of female pleasure.

It wasn't until Victorian times that the very existence of female ejaculation was formally challenged. A sexologist named Krafft-Ebing linked "excessive" female vaginal fluid to disease, and decided women who "expelled" it had some kind of pathology that was probably linked to the nervous system.

Ironically, lesbian feminist historian Sheila Jeffreys apparently interpreted all these theories as bunk and felt the notion of female ejaculation was just a figment of the male imagination.

My favourite proof of its existence, however, is Bell's description of the puberty rites of the Batoro of Uganda. She describes a custom called "kachapati," which means "spray the wall." The older women teach the younger women how to ejaculate when they reach puberty, Bell writes. It reminded me of a radio program I had once heard on this subject, in which one women described how she had "kachapatied" the paint right off the wall of her bedroom.

I've ejaculated several times since that experience in my teens. I haven't learned to control it myself the way Bell has. Sometimes, with the right circumstances and the proper stimulation, it happens. The more it does, the more I understand how to make it happen. It's not necessarily more satisfying than a clitoral orgasm, just different. I don't feel the need for it to happen every time. It's fun when it does but I don't feel cheated or like my lover is inadequate when it doesn't. The bottom line is that it happens and I have no doubt as to what it is.

Researchers and sex therapists say one of their main concerns in supporting the existence of the G-spot is that they worry it will, as the infamous sex therapist Dr. Ruth puts it, send every couple on a "Lewis and Clark expedition up her vagina." Come on, give me a break. We've still got women who aren't achieving clitoral orgasms and it's not because we are denying that the clitoris exists. Lewis and Clark didn't have a man and they didn't know what they were going to find, but that didn't stop them from exploring.

Labia Envy
Size Matters for Some Women Too

WOMEN don't tend to check out each other's labia in the locker room. Perhaps that's because we're less concerned with the size and shape of things down there than guys are.

Well, that's changing.

The aforementioned penis extender Dr. Robert H. Stubbs, a cosmetic surgeon in Toronto, also does labia reductions and female circumcisions. Before you get your knickers in a knot, the procedure is approved by the College of Physicians and Surgeons and requested by women.

"The words 'female circumcision' create all kinds of confusion and adverse reaction in the West because of increased awareness of the practice of female genital mutilation in certain cultures," says Stubbs. "But female circumcision is not the correct term for something like clitoradectomies where the entire clitoris is cut off. I go to great lengths to protect the clitoris."

Thanks, Doc.

What Stubbs does do is trim down the labia minora on women who feel they have an excess of it. The labia minora extend up over the clitoris to form the clitoral hood, and are analogous to the male foreskin. If the excess also extends over the clitoral hood, trimming it is technically called a female circumcision—a term that makes people very nervous. "When I started doing the procedure," says Stubbs, "I wanted to make sure I wouldn't have my license removed, so I wrote the College of Physicians and Surgeons (the body that licenses him) and included pictures of what I was doing: that is, shortening the labia minora up around the clitoris—technically a female circumcision.

"The lawyer/doctor at the college was flabbergasted but they acknowledged that what I was doing was appropriate."

Stubbs wasn't aware that genital shape and size could also be a female obsession until 1986 when a woman concerned about the size of her labia showed up at a public clinic where he worked. Now labia reduction has become a standard procedure at the Cosmetic Surgicentre, Stubbs' private clinic. "In the last year, I've seen a number of women concerned about the appearance of their genitals and have performed surgery on about eight or nine of them," he says.

Describing herself as a bit of a "peacock," Deborah has had her eyes done, and had breast implants and some liposuction. She started thinking about her labia when her husband brought home porn magazines and she started comparing herself. "I saw some other ones that were cuter than mine and thought, 'Hey, I want that one,'" she laughs. But it wasn't just cosmetic, Deborah is quick to add. She says the excess skin made sex less enjoyable, both physically and psychologically. It's not like her labia were dragging on the ground but, measuring in at about three-and-a-quarter centimetres, they were a little bigger than average. "There was just too much skin," explains the thirty-something woman. "I was always having to stop during sex to shift it or move it out of the way. It was a real pain."

A doctor with whom Deborah shared her concerns ten years ago told her to get over it—that the excess made things nice and "cushiony" for her lovers. Deborah was too insecure to protest. Then a couple years ago she found Stubbs. He gave her inner labia a trim, including the part that extends up over the clitoris to form the clitoral hood.

Deborah is thrilled with the results. "Look ma, no hands," she laughs, explaining what sex is like post-surgery. Stubbs says most of the women who have the procedure report more sexual pleasure. "One woman who had never had an orgasm with normal sex was suddenly becoming responsive," he says. "There wasn't contact between her and her partner because there was all this skin getting in the way."

Stubbs is careful to explain that the women coming to him for this procedure are mostly in their thirties. "They've had a chance to assess what they want in life, what they're prepared to put up with, and what they can afford. They're not young, inexperienced women out on a whim."

And he won't do the procedure for everyone. "One woman came in who'd been a professional body builder, and steroids had made her clitoris and hood to grow to the point where they almost looked like a young boy's genitalia," Stubbs explains. "She wanted me to remove her clitoris but I told her I didn't think that would be wise. I told her what I would be comfortable doing but she wasn't interested, so I didn't do the surgery."

Depending on the extent of the reduction, the procedure takes one to two hours and involves sedation and local freezing. Cost ranges from $1,500 to $2,000.

Deborah says it hurt. "It stung pretty bad for a couple of weeks," she says. "I used a lot of cream and took plenty of seltzer baths. It was a bit of a nightmare but it was worth it."

Now, before you all haul out your rulers or start getting insecure about what's things look like down there, remember that, like snowflakes and penises, no two vaginas are alike.

And that's what makes them special.

Kiss 'n' Tell
Why We Tell Our Girlfriends Everything

"WHAT EXACTLY do you say about me?" he asked during one of our Saturday-morning-in-bed information sessions.

"Uhhh, that you're the most fabulous lover I've ever had, of course."

"Yeah, right."

"No really, I do mostly rave about our sex life. Okay, sometimes I might raise an eensy, little issue here and there."

"Are you saying I'm small."

"Chill out. Of course not. I'm just saying that once in a while I might talk to her if something's troubling me about sex. It's rarely anything you and I haven't discussed already. Besides, I can't make our sex life sound too good. Some of these friends are single."

We were talking about how men and women talk to their friends about their relationships—specifically about the sex. Or more correctly, how men don't talk to their friends about their relationships—specifically not about the sex.

Whereas me, I've barely got my pants on and I'm on the blower to the girls, especially at the beginning of a relationship. "Hi, howzit going, howz work? I finally slept with Richard."

"What! Oh my God. How was it!?"

"He was very sweet. Shy, but sweet. And very, um, attentive."

"Oral?"

"Yes, excellent. Great tongue."

"Did you have intercourse?"

"Yeah, sort of."

"What do you mean, sort of?"

"Well, he kinda lost his erection when we put the condom on."

"Oh no, not one of those. Think it's chronic?"

"No, I think he was just nervous. He was cool about it. We just did other stuff."

"Size?"

"Pretty good. Been with bigger, been with smaller.'

"Gonna see him again?"

"I hope so; we had a good time. Dinner was nice. We clicked."

And that's a tame example. Most guys would never have this conversation with a male friend. I wish more of them would.

"Don't you talk to your male friends about our sex?" I asked him.

"Not really, I mean, we might talk about how much sex we're having, or what position we last longest in," he offers. "Or maybe, if we're feeling really confessional, that you wish she'd be more into oral sex, for example."

"But you wouldn't share your cunnilingus tips with your best friend."

"No."

"Why not?"

"I dunno, it seems so clinical. I once walked into a room where some women were having a graphic conversation about blow jobs," he explained. "It was a real turn-off. It made it seem so impersonal."

Most men I've gone out with learn to live with the fact that my girlfriends get all the dirt about our relationship, but that doesn't mean they like it. Some guys have even tried to stop it, "forbidding" me to talk about our sex life to my friends. As if. Most guys have learned better. They know they have to live with it, but it still makes them squirm not knowing just how much my girlfriends know.

I do agree that there is such a thing as too much information. I don't really need to picture my girlfriend's boyfriend handcuffed, tied from the ceiling, clad in her favourite bra and panties. It might make me a little uncomfy next time we all go out to the movies together. You have to know where to draw the line.

But it's worth learning where that line is (after years of practice, it becomes second nature). There's too much valuable information there not to. Whether it's for advice, tips or just for the sheer pleasure of living vicariously through a friend's particularly raucous sexual experience, talking to your girlfriends about your sex life can be tremendously useful. It's a chance to gush, especially early on when you're not ready to let him know the extent of your feelings. Spilling your guts to a girlfriend can help channel some of your excitement so you don't spill it onto the relationship before he can handle it. A girlfriend can also put things into perspective and remind you of your short-term memory: "You said the exact same thing about Peter," when you proclaim, "I reeeally feel like this one is different."

Later on in the relationship, talking to a girlfriend about your sex life is good for test-running a discussion topic before you bring it up with him. By bouncing your thoughts off a friend, you sort out your feelings, figure out if there are solutions you could exercise on your own, and come up with the best way to raise the issue with him. If there are sexual problems, your girlfriend may have had a similar experience and can share how she dealt with it. Knowing she's been through the same thing can also help to normalize a situation so you don't get too freaked out by it. Very reassuring.

Often, we don't even have to go into graphic detail. Experiences are common enough that much of the discussion can be handled in code. "Oh, another number five—don't worry honey, me and Johnny just went through a number five."

It's easier early on, when things are less intimate and you're less concerned about the guy's feelings. As the two of you get closer, you develop a little more respect for his privacy and tend to share a little less with your girlfriends. (They usually have most of the vital information by then anyway.) Also, as you get closer, you share more with your partner, so there is less of a need to go elsewhere for advice. Besides, after you're with someone for a while, your sex life takes on its own unique complexity and loses some of the universality that makes it so much fun to share with friends.

Sometimes it's more fun to keep it to yourself, or yourselves. There's an excitement in knowing that there are things only the two of you share, especially sexually.

Still, no matter how long I'm with someone, there's no way I could ever keep my girlfriends in the dark entirely. I admit, though, that I don't think I'd be too comfortable knowing that all his friends know what it takes to get me off, or what my favourite position is.

That's not to say, however, I still wouldn't mind if guys compared a few more notes now and then.

Ouch!

Sometimes Sex Can Be a Real Pain

SEX CAN BE A REAL PAIN sometimes. In fact, in one couple's case, sex was such a pain that it finally caused the break-up of their ten year relationship.

Some studies say up to 50 percent of women experience painful intercourse—doctors call it dyspareunia—at some point in their lives. I guess it's not surprising, really, when you consider all that goes on up there. But for 10 to 15 percent of women, this pain is chronic. It hurts every time.

This wouldn't be so bad, I suppose. It might force him to expand his sexual repertoire. The problem, according to Sophie Bergeron—a third-year graduate student in clinical psychology at McGill University—is that once you make the intercourse = pain connection, it's usually not long before your whole interest in sex takes a nose-dive. Even as a kid you only had to get burned once to learn not to touch the hot stove.

Bergeron is studying a type of dyspareunia called vulvar vestibulitis syndrome (VVS). (Where do they get these names?) Apparently, some women's vulvic area (the pearly gates, if you will) gets super sensitive, and trying to stick anything up there can cause extreme pain. Understandably, sex stops being a very desirable activity.

"Since intercourse is painful, the impact this has is that it cuts off arousal and desire," explains Bergeron. "Eventually they don't want to have anything to do with sex or even masturbation. If they do engage in sex, it's often for their partner's sake and the women don't really enjoy it themselves."

In some cases, the anticipation or fear of pain can cause a woman's vagina to tense or clam up entirely—a condition known as vaginismus. Naturally, things get tense in the relationship as well. Sometimes it's enough to break it up.

Even though VVS (pain deep in the vagina during intercourse is another type of dyspareunia) was first documented over a century ago, doctors are still pretty clueless about it. A regular gynecological exam won't necessarily detect it (though if it's really red at the entrance and she hits the roof when a cotton swab touches it, that might be the first clue). And you know how doctors can be. If they can't see anything unusual and all tests are negative there's only one explanation for your seemingly inexplicable complaints about painful intercourse: It's all in your head. After hearing that a few times, you stop complaining. Eventually you might even start believing it. And chances are your partner has already come to this conclusion. It's easier than thinking the problem might have something to do with him, like, what if it's because she's no longer attracted to him?

The truth is, they don't really know what causes VVS. About

50 percent of women suffer from it right from the first time they have intercourse, says Bergeron. The rest develop it over the course of their sexual life. Theories involve chronic yeast infections, or perhaps an allergic reaction to the chemical-laden creams that treat them. Venereal warts and urinary-tract infections are suspect as well.

Of course, if you do get a doctor to believe you, guess what the most popular treatment is? That's right—surgery. They put you under, shave a couple millimetres of tissue off your vulva, and replace it with some of the less-sensitive skin from inside your vagina.

Bergeron says women tend to opt for surgery because they see it as a quick fix. "But the problem with surgery is that while it may take away the pain, the women might still be stuck with their desire and arousal problems so that their sex life is not necessarily better."

With this study, she is comparing the success of surgery to less invasive treatments like behavioural and sex therapy, relaxation, and biofeedback. These demand more time and personal investment, Bergeron admits, but she thinks the results may be worth it.

Biofeedback works with a small sensor that is inserted into the vagina like a tampon. The sensor's cord is plugged into a computer that displays the level of tension in the vaginal muscles. "We find the muscles to be more spastic and tense for these women," Bergeron explains. "Once this tension is monitored we can work on a series of contractions and relaxation techniques to take away the pain."

Pain management is a third treatment option offered in groups of five or six women (which is also helpful since most women feel like they're the only ones with this problem). The group learns a combination of relaxation and pain-management techniques combined with sex therapy to try and renew desire. "We try to deal with the anxiety and frustration these women feel along with the problems they may be experiencing with their partner," she says. "We help them be more assertive with their partner, increase their comfort with their genitals, and their knowledge about sexuality."

Sounds like something most women gotta work through. True enough, Bergeron admits. In fact, studies have shown that women with VVS have no more psychological problems than women who don't experience pain. But toss the pain factor into the regular mix, and before you know it a simple caress from your partner can make you freak out.

That's not that same as saying it's all in your head. "Because these women have been told so often that it's all in their head, we are very careful not to reinforce that notion," says Bergeron. "What we try to do is stop the association of pain with sex and renew the association of sex with pleasure."

Get that into your head.

I Love Trash

Why Women Love Romance Novels

"I rammed it in, and, in two strokes, I shot my load deep inside, just as Carla came with a tremendous shudder."

—Penthouse Forum

"When finally the moment came when they did not pull back, it was as if the world dropped out from under them in a sudden blinding flash, and left them to fall fearlessly through time and space while they celebrated the wonder of each other."

—Harlequin Romance

UH, YA... and we wonder why men and women have such different takes on sex. Compare our resource material.

Of course, none of the women I know read romance novels. Pure trash, we huff, noses in the air. Just as only slimy loser-guys with paunches read Penthouse, only women who wear bad polyester pantsuits read romance novels, right? So how do you explain the fact that women spend $885 million a year on them, according to the folks at *The Romantic Times*, a monthly magazine devoted to the subject of romance novels? The mag, which has 150,000 subscribers, reviews the 120 new titles that come out every month (yes, 120, three times the number when the mag started in 1981) and keeps people abreast of what's up in this fantasy world. They even sponsor an annual convention for romance novel readers.

It was time to see what the fuss was about. I picked up three (at $5 or $6 bucks a pop, romance novels even share the same cover price as Penthouse) and sailed through all of them in a week. Just research, of course. Truth is, they are trash, cheesy, totally ridiculous, girl meets boy, makes him fall painfully and deeply in love with her, everything-works-out-the-way-you-want-it-to trash. Smutty too in a let-me-explore-your-peaks-and-valleys way. I admit it. I loved them. I may even get more.

Well, what's not to love? I'm (I mean, she's) beautiful, he's hunky, and when we make love, he's always exploring crooks and hollows in my body and lavishing me with affection and constantly taking me to the limits of sexual tension before he eventually takes me over. And we always live happily ever after.

Sure, the scenarios are ridiculous and the writing, well... but when you break it down, you start to understand the appeal. Tami M. Bereska, who teaches in the sociology department at the University of Alberta, takes romance novels seriously. When she discovered that, in 1989, women bought 7,000 Harlequins an hour, she decided the phenomenon warranted some study. Bereska thinks that, first and foremost, romance novels are a great escape. "Women are still nurturers, we are taught to take care of others, whether as secretaries, nurses, wives, mothers," Bereska explains. "In romance novels, the heroine is nurtured by the hero, she gets taken care of for once. Women are nurtured vicariously through her."

They also individualize our problems, Bereska believes. "The heroines usually encounter some arrogant, gorgeous hunk who can't express his feelings [nah, never happens to me…], but rather than suggesting that it is the result of a social problem requiring social change, the problems in the novel are solved by the heroine individually, within her own relationship. She's able to change him so that in the end he realizes how deeply he loves her."

Now that's what I call fantasy! Mind you, it's no more far-fetched than a guy whose ideal woman greets him every night at the door dressed in sexy lingerie and is ready to please him all night long.

The constant buildup is what got me. All those arm hairs brushing and hearts leaping and dropping left and right. I'm such a sucker for melodrama.

In fact, Bereska informs me, the formula sheets publishers send to potential authors dictate how many pages should be devoted to each sex scene, how much of the description should focus on the act itself and how much on build-up. "Guidelines are very strict and vary from series to series," says Bereska. "These change over time, however, since publishers do extensive market research to find out what their readers want."

The virginal nineteen-year-old heroine of the 70s has become the independent, educated, professional babe in her late twenties who's no longer at the mercy of her man. That doesn't mean hunkman has turned into a wimp. He still has to be stronger than she is so she can melt into his golden, rippling arms and he can protect her, but he's no longer expected to provide for her materially. Basically, it's the same old woman needs a man to be complete message but with some modern twists.

Content changes have changed the readership. No longer the domain of bored housewives, readers now cut across the demographic spectrum, says Bereska.

From my friend's grandmother, much to his discomfort ("I just have a hard time thinking about her reading the dirty bits," he tells me), to thirty-year-old sex columnists, to Texas cowboys. (One statistic showed Texas to have the highest percentage of male readership. Go figure.)

Romance novels make up about 48 percent of total paperback fiction sales in the U.S. (60-80 percent of all new titles are from Harlequin), meaning romance novel writers make a bundle if they're good.

But this is a female-dominated field. Women don't buy, it seems, with a male author's name on the cover. Some guys use pseudonyms to get around this but even this doesn't always work, says Bereska. "Women readers have told me they can tell if it's been written by a man by the sex scenes," she says. "They're cruder, more physical, less emotional, and more focused on her than about her."

Husband/wife teams are also common (as a way to get it right from both sides, I suppose), adds Bereska. "One husband/wife team gave up their law firm to go into writing romance novels full time. The money was better." Needless to say, and before you get any ideas, competition has gotten tough. Gone are the days of unsolicited manuscripts. These days, you need an agent and a reputation.

Trash? Maybe, but it's worth sorting through, says Bereska. "Romance novels have a lot to tell us about female desire and what women are looking for in their lives."

I have to admit that we certainly concern ourselves enough with how male wank material perpetuates men's ideas about sex, so it makes sense to give the other side a good going over. Especially since women are mountain-climbing and hang gliding during sex while men are doing the 100-yard-dash.

Dew Me!
Smut for Girls

PORN FOR STRAIGHT GIRLS is in a sorry state. Either we slog through pages of politically correct rape fantasies or indulge our same-sex fantasies and resort to beaver shots of airbrushed women standing on their head. And as for naked boys, what do we have? Playgirl? Yeah, well, whatever—gay porn disguised as straight-girl porn. Like I said, porn for straight girls is in a sorry state. Perhaps I should be patient; "women's erotica" is really just going through puberty. And we're still stuck in this belief that women aren't visual, women like a story, women want a plot, yada, yada, yada…. I don't know about you, but my arm gets sore turning the pages through all that plot.

Regardless, whether it's because it's all so new, or we're still feeling guilty, or I'm just superficial, it does seem that women would still rather read erotic stories than look at dirty pictures. "In the last few years we've seen a real boom in women's erotic fiction," says Joanne Cadorette, the owner of L'Androgyne bookstore in Montreal. "I think it's partly because it's less taboo to talk about feminism and pornography in the same sentence. Women are becoming more accepting of their sexuality."

Susie Bright pretty much got the "women's erotica" ball rolling

Josey Vogels

with the *Herotica* anthologies. In fact, *Herotica* 1, 2, 3 and 4 are still among the bestsellers in women's erotica. But still, and not that I mind so much, these anthologies are a grab bag of sexual orientations. And usually the more hardcore stuff is lesbian oriented. For straight women, even though some are beginning to admit they might like decent porn—excuse me, erotica—it seems you still have to package it differently for them to buy it. In other words, you have to make it boring.

"Women's erotica is still marketed much more as 'literature' than porn," says Cadorette.

Or as porn disguised as trashy romance novels. Series of erotic novels like Black Lace, Masquerade, Headline Delta and X Libris look pretty much like Harlequins with slightly more out-of-focus covers. Except you won't find any romance, says Montreal writer Sylvie Ouellette, while working on her third title for Black Lace. "These are not love stories," she says. "They're sexual adventures—an extended fantasy, so to speak. There is no emphasis on the relationship aspect, no boy meets girl." But they still rely on formula. Britain's Black Lace cranks out two new titles every month and has well over 100 titles available in 32 countries and 14 languages. They too, like most romance publishers, have writer guidelines and only accept manuscripts from women.

Ouellette describes what Black Lace thinks is the difference between what men and women want when it comes to their wank material. "If you write for a male readership, you'll be much more concerned with describing what's going on, more like a voyeur,"

My Messy Bedroom ◆◆◆

Ouellette explains. "Whereas writing for women you have to get much more inside the characters' minds and describe what they feel as it's happening. It's not enough to say, 'He put her hand on his penis and he kissed her somewhere between the legs.' You have to say something like 'She feels his excitement as he's caressing her,' or that 'she can feel the heat of arousal.'"

Things also have to be more polite.

"You can be explicit but not vulgar," says Ouellette. "Four-letter words are allowed but not as a conjugated verb." In other words, she could say "I'd like to fuck him" but could not say "He took her panties off and fucked her." Which creates its own challenge, she admits. "You have to find different ways of describing the same things, and it can get repetitious."

You're telling me! In reading her first Black Lace novel, *Healing Passions*, I felt like I was gonna scream if any more "dew" flowed. Never mind that I have never, ever called anything that "flowed" between my legs "dew."

Black Lace guidelines also make sure there's a little bit of something for everyone: some bondage, a few same-sex scenes (though there are no male/male scenes unless she's watching or participating). As well, the main character is always a woman, the women always get off and they have the right to say no. Hell, maybe it's not so bad.

But it is bad. Cheesy and bad. Like most of the so-called women-oriented crap out there.

"Because women's erotica is fairly new as a genre, a lot of it is bad and that's something that people are just starting to admit," says Carol Queen, a sex educator who does erotic-writing workshops in San Francisco. "Part of the problem is that it started out as more of a political point. It was important to get erotic material by and for women out there and make it accessible for all women. As a result, all kinds of women were submitting erotic stories but they weren't necessarily very well written."

Once the floodgates opened (or the dew started flowing, if you like), publishers scrambled to get material out there, slapping anything together and sticking the words "women" and "erotica" on the cover. That's because the term "women's erotica" usually means "safe"—which means people, men included, who don't want to admit they like smut feel okay about buying it. And unlike *Penthouse* or *Hustler,* you can buy it in major bookstores.

It's obvious that men too are looking for an alternative to the pussy parade of straight-male porn. "I've heard from a lot of women who read my book who say that their husbands don't want to read it because it's 'women's stuff,'" says Ouelette, "but if the woman reads it too him aloud, he's like, 'Hey, read some more.'"

So much for "women's" erotica. In fact, getting away from this whole notion of gender-specific porn might be just the cure for the sorry state of straight porn. Maybe it's less a question of male or female porn than one of good porn. Maybe we could just depict sex, real sex, with no flowery fields, no flowing dew, no big hair.

I think part of my problem is that I don't know what I want. I just know I haven't found it yet.

Chicks Tell All

Everything You Ever Wanted to Know About Women

WELL, GUYS, here it is: Everything you always wanted to know about women but were afraid to ask. Compiled from guys who really want to know, for example…

What's it like to have breasts?

The novelty wears off by the time we're about fifteen. I think it coincides with our first gym class with boobs. Then they're mostly a pain in the ass: finding the right bra for them, having guys direct entire conversations at them, having kids (and men) gnaw on them, then watching them fall victim to gravity. They can be fun to dress up or push up. It's also fun to have someone run their fingers and lips all over them once in awhile (just remember, they are not toys to be tweaked, squished or poked whenever you feel like it). To get an idea, strap a couple pieces of round fruit (large oranges are about a C-cup, cantaloupe a D-cup) on your chest for a day and see how it feels.

Why does it takes you so long to come?

Most sex books clock the male orgasm at about three to five

minutes from erection, while women need at least seven to ten minutes from arousal to orgasm. Other factors to consider: women usually get a later start on figuring out the orgasm thing as young'uns. We're also easily distracted—sometimes by you being concerned about how long it's taking us to come. And the mechanics just are not as simple with us. Sometimes you gotta prop up the hood and spend some time getting to know the engine, if you know what I mean.

Do you really fake it sometimes? And if so, why?

Yes, we've all faked it. But most of us eventually realize it's a waste of time and energy. Sorry, but even your ego isn't worth it. Besides, it inevitably backfires when we realize we have to make the real thing live up to prior performances so we don't get caught. A trained professional will know the difference. If she jumps up immediately afterwards and starts cleaning the windows or organizing her closet, she probably faked it. If she lies there limply with a stupid dazed look and a shit-eating grin on her face, give yourself a pat on the back. As for why we fake it, well... the aforementioned ego, boredom and, once again, our concern that you are concerned that we are taking too long.

What does it feel like to have a period?

Imagine having air injected into your abdomen along with some shards of glass. Add a steady, dull ache and the occasional warm gush that feels like you just wet yourself, and that pretty much covers it. Oh yeah, sometimes it smells bad, too.

How come we can't blame your manic behaviour and inexplicable tears on PMS but you can?

See, just because our manic behaviour might be explained by PMS, it might not be. That's our call. If you make the call, any legitimate bad feelings are undermined thus making us want to slug you. Besides, since we have to suffer most of our lives with our period (see above), we get to make all the rules about it.

Why is intuition a female thing?

It just is. I can sense it.

What's your big beef with testosterone?

"It's like garlic to a vampire," one guy complained. "Women are always blaming shit on testosterone." Men have more testosterone and display proportionately more obnoxious, aggressive behaviour. You do the math. Admittedly, the too-much-testosterone explanation is becoming a bit cliché, and I've been told, in fact, that the hormone is sometimes used to subdue overly aggressive behaviour. Perhaps we should let this one go and just blame stupid macho behaviour on men.

Who made women the experts on relationships?

Why, we did, of course. Pretty smart, eh? Chalk it up to female intuition, but, quite simply, sometimes you guys just don't get it.

If you would only see things our way, it really would make things a whole lot easier.

Why can you objectify a man's body but get upset when we comment on how hot some chick is?

Thousands of years of history. Don't get me started.

Why do you ask if you look fat in an outfit when you don't really want to know?

Yeah, that one's pretty much a no-win situation. If you say no, we think you're lying. If you say yes, you're dead. The best way to avoid this is to tell us we look great at all times.

How can you love shopping that much?

As a full-fledged shopaholic, I like to think of shopping as more of an ongoing daily quest for the ultimate deal on the ultimate outfit. Each discovery is an achievement, each major score a skilled accomplishment. And yes, we really do need another pair of shoes.

Why do you go to the bathroom in pairs?

So she can hand us some toilet paper under the stall because we have, once again picked the one with no paper. That, and because we must find out who each other wants to sleep with outside the bathroom and sort out any overlap so things don't get ugly later.

Do you really enjoy giving oral sex?

As long as you let us control the rhythm and speed and don't start thrusting it down our throat, fellatio is fun. It helps if you don't smell like an old sock too.

Why do you get annoyed when we do nice things for you after you've asked why we don't do nice things for you more?

Because we know you're only doing it because we told you. The trick is to not have to be asked; but if you must be asked, then the trick is to wait until we forget we asked and surprise us.

Why is it that when you want to talk about something we don't want to talk about you bug us until we talk about it, but when you don't want to talk about something we're supposed to respect that?

I don't want to talk about it.